Poems of the Decade

An anthology of the
Forward Books of Poetry

T0322943

Poems of the Decade

An anthology of the
Forward Books of Poetry

**Forward
Prizes
for Poetry**

First published in Great Britain by
Forward Arts Foundation,
in association with
Faber & Faber · Bloomsbury House · 74-77 Great Russell Street
London WC1B 3DA

ISBN 978 0 571 36941 6 (paperback)

Compilation copyright © Forward Arts Foundation 2021
Permissions cleared by Suzanne Fairless-Aitken – Swift Permissions
(swiftpermissions@gmail.com)
Preface copyright © William Sieghart
Cover copyright © Keith Hau

Typeset by Avon DataSet Ltd, Alcester, Warwickshire B49 6HN
Printed and bound by CPI Group (UK), Croydon CR0 4YY

A CIP catalogue reference for this book

is available at the British Library

1 3 5 7 9 10 8 6 4 2

To Susannah Herbert

Contents

Preface

This collection of poems is a distillation of ten years' worth of entries to the annual Forward Prizes for Poetry. While being an entirely personal selection, it represents contributions from the winners and shortlisted poets in the three prize-winning categories: Best Collection, Best First Collection and Best Single Poem, with some outstanding additions from the annual Forward Books of Poetry. No poet features more than once, allowing one hundred different voices to express their poetic thoughts across these pages. Their concerns and inspirations cover the gamut of the lives and the world we have inhabited over the past decade.

In some ways, it seems that poetry always gets there first amongst the art forms – requiring as it does nothing but a pen or a keyboard – and, in our intricately connected world, the capacity to share those carefully wrought words with audiences in every nook and cranny of the planet means that poetry is more widely communicated than ever. The broadening of these voices and their origins over the past decade has been the single most remarkable feature of how poetry has evolved around us. Stimulated by the spread of social media, the narrow funnel through which poetry has traditionally been published and appreciated has been transformed, and publishers are eagerly pursuing poets with their own audiences, changing the paths and possibilities for poets and poetry alike. This also accentuates poetry's immediate relevance to our existence and its booming popularity. More people read, write, share and buy poetry than ever before, and after spending many privileged months trying to distil over twelve hundred poems into the chosen hundred for this collection, it was not hard to understand why.

The range of subject material, experiences and emotions that these poems cover also makes you aware of the immediacy of the art form. This decade of poetry began when Barack Obama entered the White House and ended before the arrival of coronavirus in our lives. Yet, as you absorb the hundred poems in this book, you will see how they deal with the day-to-day dramas in our lives, not just the traditional subjects of life and death, parents and children, love and loss but also the minute complexities of modern 21st-century living and the new challenges they entail. I hope you find a connection with some of the poems in this collection and many that will intrigue, inspire and reward you. As a way of looking at the world and the last ten years in our lives, in my mind, this anthology can't be rivalled.

It has been an absolute privilege and a blessing to make this selection, particularly in a year of lockdown, and I'm very grateful to the poets and judges from ten years of the Forward Prizes who have given us so much to absorb and reflect upon. I hope this anthology gives you as much pleasure to read as it gave me to select.

William Sieghart
Founder of the Forward Prizes for Poetry
May 2021

www.forwardartsfoundation.org
@forwardprizes

Poems of the Decade

An anthology of the
Forward Books of Poetry

Patience Agbabi

The Doll's House

The source of the wealth that built Harewood is historical fact. There is nothing anyone can do to change the past, however appalling or regrettable that past might be. What we can do, however, what we must do, is engage with that legacy and in so doing stand a chance of having a positive effect on the future. David Lascelles

Art is a lie that makes us realise truth. Pablo Picasso

Welcome to my house, this stately home
where, below stairs, my father rules as chef:
confecting, out of sugar-flesh and -bone,
décor so fine, your tongue will treble clef
singing its name. Near-sighted and tone-deaf,
I smell-taste-touch; create each replica
in my mind's tongue. My name? Angelica.

This is my world, the world of haute cuisine:
high frosted ceilings, modelled on high art,
reflected in each carpet's rich design;
each bed, each armchair listed à la carte.
Come, fellow connoisseur of taste, let's start
below stairs, where you'll blacken your sweet tooth,
sucking a beauty whittled from harsh truth...

Mind your step! The stairway's worn and steep,
let your sixth senses merge in the half-light...
This muted corridor leads to the deep
recesses of the house. Here, to your right,
my father's realm of uncurbed appetite –
private! The whiff of strangers breaks his spell.
Now left, to the dead end. Stop! Can you smell

cinnamon, brown heat in the afternoon
of someone else's summer? This rust key
unlocks the passage to my tiny room,
stick-cabin, sound-proofed with a symphony
of cinnamon; shrine to olfactory
where I withdraw to paint in cordon bleu,
shape, recreate this house; in miniature.

All art is imitation: I'm a sculptor
of past-imperfect; hungry, I extract
molasses; de- and reconstruct high culture
from base material; blend art and fact
in every glazed and glistening artefact
housed in this doll's house. Stately home of sugar.
Of Demerara cubes secured with nougat.

Look at its hall bedecked with royal icing –
the ceiling's crossbones mirrored in the frieze,
the chimneypiece. The floor is sugar glazing
clear as a frozen lake. My centrepiece
statue of Eve, what a creative feast!
A crisp Pink Lady, sculpted with my teeth,
its toffee glaze filming the flesh beneath.

The music room's my favourite. I make music
by echoing design: the violet-rose
piped ceiling is the carpet's fine mosaic
of granulated violet and rose,
aimed to delight the eye, the tongue, the nose.
Even the tiny chairs are steeped in flavour
delicate as a demisemiquaver.

Taste, if you like, sweet as a mothertongue…
See how this bedroom echoes my refrain:
the chairs, the secretaire, commode, chaise longue,
four-poster bed, all carved from sugarcane;

even the curtains that adorn its frame,
chiselled from the bark, each lavish fold
drizzled with tiny threads of spun 'white gold'.

The library was hardest. How to forge
each candied volume wafer-thin, each word
burnt sugar. In the midnight hours, I'd gorge
on bubbling syrup, mouth its language; learned
the temperature at which burnt sugar burned,
turned sweet to bitter; inked a tiny passage
that overflowed into a secret passage,

the Middle Passage; made definitive
that muted walkway paved with sugar plate,
its sugar-paper walls hand-painted with
hieroglyphs invisible as sweat
but speaking volumes; leading to the sweet
peardrop of a stairwell down and down
to this same room of aromatic brown

in miniature. Here, connoisseur, I've set
the doll, rough hewn from sugarcane's sweet wood:
her choker, hardboiled sweets as black as jet;
her dress, molasses-rich; her features, hard.
This handcarved doll, with sugar in her blood –
Europe, the Caribbean, Africa;
baptised in sugar, named Angelica,

has built a tiny house in Demerara
sugar grains secured with sugarpaste,
each sculpted room a microscopic mirror
of its old self; and below stairs, she's placed
a blind doll with kaleidoscopic taste,
who boils, bakes, moulds, pipes, chisels, spins and blows
sugar, her art, the only tongue she knows.

Mir Mahfuz Ali

Hurricane

A storm roared over the Bay of Bengal,
a glass bull charging with its horns.
It pounded throughout the long night
as we children huddled together

inside our fatherless bungalow.
We watched our tin roof rip off.
First from its tie beams
then the ceiling joists. One by one

the rest of the house vanished
as we covered our heads with our hands
and saw our possessions take flight –
The *Koran*, *War and Peace*, *Gitanjali*,

the clothes in the alna, shoes and sandals,
sisters' dolls and brothers' cricket bats.
We children couldn't understand
what sins we'd committed,

but we asked God's forgiveness.
We thought the worst was over.
Then came the giant waves
one after the other snatching us

from the arms of our mother,
tossing us like cheap wood.
Trees fell, exposing their great roots.
Cats and cattle lay dead on the ground.

Our bodies shrivelled with water,
shuddered like old engines.
Teeth rattled to the point of rapture.
The sun came very late that day,

found us trapped in a wind-sheared tree.
We couldn't hear the birds singing
or the muezzin calling for prayer. Silence,
the new disease, swept across our land.

Raymond Antrobus

The Perseverance

Love is the man overstanding
                    Peter Tosh

I wait outside THE PERSEVERANCE.
Just popping in here a minute.
I'd heard him say it many times before
like all kids with a drinking father,
watch him disappear
into smoke and laughter.

There is no such thing as too much laughter,
my father says, drinking in THE PERSEVERANCE
until everything disappears —
I'm outside counting minutes,
waiting for the man, my *father*
to finish his shot and take me home before

it gets dark. We've been here before,
no such thing as too much laughter
unless you're my mother without my father,
working weekends while THE PERSEVERANCE
spits him out for a minute.
He gives me 50p to make me disappear.

50p in my hand, I disappear
like a coin in a parking meter before
the time runs out. How many minutes
will I lose listening to the laughter
spilling from THE PERSEVERANCE
while strangers ask, *where is your father?*

I stare at the doors and say, *my father
is working*. Strangers who don't disappear
but hug me for my perseverance.
Dad said *this will be the last time* before,
while the TV spilled canned laughter,
us, on the sofa in his council flat, knowing any minute

the yams will boil, any minute,
I will eat again with my father,
who cooks and serves laughter
good as any Jamaican who disappeared
from the Island I tasted before
overstanding our heat and perseverance.

I still hear *popping in for a minute*, see him disappear.
We lose our fathers before we know it.
I am still outside THE PERSEVERANCE, listening for the laughter.

Simon Armitage

Poundland

Came we then to the place abovementioned,
crossed its bristled threshold through robotic glass doors,
entered its furry heat, its flesh-toned fluorescent light.
Thus with wire-wrought baskets we voyaged,
and some with trolleys, back wheels flipping like trout tails,
cruised the narrow canyons twixt cascading shelves,
the prow of our journeying cleaving stale air.
Legion were the items that came tamely to hand:
five stainless steel teaspoons, ten corn-relief plasters,
the busy bear pedal bin liners fragranced with country lavender,
the Disney design calendar and diary set, three cans of Vimto,
cornucopia of potato-based snacks and balm for a sweet tooth,
toys and games, goods of Orient made, and of Cathay,
all under the clouded eye of CCTV,
beyond the hazard cone where serious chutney spillage had occurred.
Then emerged souls: the duty manager with a face like Doncaster,
mumbling, 'For so much, what shall we give in return?'
The blood-stained employee of the month,
sobbing on a woolsack of fun-fur rugs,
many uniformed servers, spectral, drifting between aisles.
Then came Elpenor, our old friend Elpenor,
slumped and shrunken by the Seasonal Products display.
In strangled words I managed,
    'How art thou come to these shady channels, into hell's ravine?'
And he:
    'To loan sharks I owe/the bone and marrow of my all.'
Then Walt Whitman, enquiring politely of the delivery boy.
And from Special Occasions came forth Tiresias,
dead in life, alive in death, cider-scented and sock-less,
Oxfam-clad, shaving cuts to both cheeks, quoting the stock exchange.
And my own mother reaching out, slipping a tin of stewing steak
to the skirt pocket of her wedding dress,
blessed with a magician's touch, practised in need.

But never until the valley widened at the gated brink
did we open our lips to fish out those corn-coloured coins,
those minted obols, hard won tokens graced with our monarch's head,
kept hidden beneath the tongue's eel, blood-tasting,
both ornament and safeguard, of armour made.
And paid forthwith, then broke surface
and breathed extraordinary daylight into starved lungs,
steered for home through precincts and parks scalded by polar winds,
laden with whatnot, lightened of golden quids.

Mona Arshi

What Every Girl Should Know Before Marriage

after Sujata Bhatt

Eliminating thought verbs is the key to a successful marriage.

You're better off avoiding the reach for specificity and
curbing your interest in the interior of things.

The cobra always reverts to TYPE, tuneless
girls tend to wither on the vine.

Oil of jasmine will arouse river fish.

In the poetry of the Sung Dynasty the howling of monkeys
in gorges was used to express profound desolation.

Things you should have a good working knowledge
of: mitochondria, Roman roads, field glasses, making
rice (using the evaporation method only).

When your mother in law calls you smart,
it's not meant as a compliment.

The lighter her eyes, the further she'll travel.

Always have saffron in your kitchen cupboard
(but on no account ever use it).

*Taunt the sky during the day; the stars
will be your hazard at night.*

Do not underestimate the art of small talk. Learn some stock phrases such as 'they say Proust was an insufferable hypochondriac' or 'I'm confident that the Government will discharge their humanitarian obligations.'

Fasting sharpens the mind and is therefore a good time to practise reverse flight.

Your husband may not know you cheated with shop-bought *garam masala* but God will know.

Fatimah Asghar

Partition

you're kashmiri until they burn your home. take your orchards.
stake a different flag. until no one remembers the road that
brings you back. you're indian until they draw a border through
punjab. until the british captains spit *paki* as they sip your chai,
add so much foam you can't taste home. you're seraiki until your
mouth fills with english. you're pakistani until your classmates
ask what that is. then you're indian again. or *some kind of spanish*.
you speak a language until you don't. until you only recognize
it between your auntie's lips. your father was fluent in four
languages. you're illiterate in the tongues of your father. your
grandfather wrote persian poetry on glasses. maybe. you can't
remember. you made it up. someone lied. you're a daughter until
they bury your mother. until you're not invited to your father's
funeral. you're a virgin until you get too drunk. you're muslim
until you're not a virgin. you're pakistani until they start throwing
acid. you're muslim until it's too dangerous. you're safe until
you're alone. you're american until the towers fall. until there's
a border on your back.

Fiona Benson

Eurofighter Typhoon

My daughters are playing outside with plastic hoops;
the elder is trying to hula, over and over –
it falls off her hips, but she keeps trying,
and the younger is watching and giggling,
and they're happy in the bright afternoon.
I'm indoors at the hob with the door open
so I can see them, because the elder might trip,
and the younger is still a baby and liable to eat dirt,
when out of clear skies a jet comes in low
over the village. At the first muted roar
the elder runs in squealing then stops in the kitchen,
her eyes adjusting to the dimness, looking foolish
and unsure. I drop the spoon and bag of peas
and leave her frightened and tittering, wiping my hands
on my jeans, trying to walk and not run,
because I don't want to scare the baby
who's still sat on the patio alone, looking for her sister,
bewildered, trying to figure why she's gone –
all this in the odd, dead pause of the lag –
then sound catches up with the plane
and now its grey belly's right over our house
with a metallic, grinding scream
like the sky's being chainsawed open
and the baby's face drops to a square of pure fear,
she tips forward and flattens her body on the ground
and presses her face into the concrete slab.
I scoop her up and she presses in shuddering,
screaming her strange, *halt* pain cry
and it's all right now I tell her again and again,
but it's never all right now – Christ have mercy –
my daughter in my arms can't steady me –
always some woman is running to catch up her children,
we dig them out of the rubble in parts like plaster dolls –
Mary Mother of God have mercy, mercy on us all.

Tara Bergin

Stag-Boy

He enters the carriage with a roar –
he clatters in wildly and fills up the carriages with heat,
running through the train, staining the floor
with hooves dirty from the street;
tearing at the ceilings with his new branched horns,
banging his rough sides against the seats and
the women, who try to look away: Gallant!
He sings hard from his throat,
his young belling tearing at his chest,
pushing at his boy-throat.

Stag-boy –

train's noise hums in his ears,
sharp and high like crickets pulsing
in the tall grass,
and he wounds it with his horns,
maddened like a stung bull,
pushing up his head,
pushing up his mouth for his mother's teat:
Where is her beestings?
Where is the flowered mug she used to warm his milk in?

No good, no good now.

He's smashing out of the train door,
he's banging his hooves in the industrial air,
he's galloping through the city squares,
and drinking from a vandalised spring –

And still his mother walks through the house,
crying: *Stag-boy, oh stag-boy come home!*

Emily Berry

Aura

```
Listen to me              little water
I called you up    believing something
would arise            in me believing
I could make             you reappear
on my way              to the cemetery
every face was               luminous
as if they knew       something about
the dark                      I think you
were in us all         reminding me not
to despair or if         despairing know
that we did not         lose each other
either side               of the calamity
we fused                   you went inside
& I could not                    see you
but afterwards              afterwards
I could see                underwater I
could see in the dark       I could see
with my eyes closed  I could see past
the shimmer that separates the living
& the dead I knew there was nothing
no separation                it was just
aura the most               remarkable
sadness &                if only I would
keep looking             I would see you
```

Liz Berry

The Republic of Motherhood

I crossed the border into the Republic of Motherhood
and found it a queendom, a wild queendom.
I handed over my clothes and took its uniform,
its dressing gown and undergarments, a cardigan
soft as a creature, smelling of birth and milk,
and I lay down in Motherhood's bed, the bed I had made
but could not sleep in, for I was called at once to work
in the factory of Motherhood. The owl shift,
the graveyard shift. Feedingcleaninglovingfeeding.
I walked home, heartsore, through pale streets,
the coins of Motherhood singing in my pockets.
Then I soaked my spindled bones
in the chill municipal baths of Motherhood,
watching strands of my hair float from my fingers.
Each day I pushed my pram through freeze and blossom
down the wide boulevards of Motherhood
where poplars bent their branches to stroke my brow.
I stood with my sisters in the queues of Motherhood –
the weighing clinic, the supermarket – waiting
for Motherhood's bureaucracies to open their doors.
As required, I stood beneath the flag of Motherhood
and opened my mouth although I did not know the anthem.
When darkness fell I pushed my pram home again,
and by lamplight wrote urgent letters of complaint
to the Department of Motherhood but received no response.
I grew sick and was healed in the hospitals of Motherhood
with their long-closed isolation wards
and narrow beds watched over by a fat moon.
The doctors were slender and efficient
and when I was well they gave me my pram again
so I could stare at the daffodils in the parks of Motherhood
while winds pierced my breasts like silver arrows.
In snowfall, I haunted Motherhood's cemeteries,

the sweet fallen beneath my feet –
Our Lady of the Birth Trauma, Our Lady of Psychosis.
I wanted to speak to them, tell them I understood,
but the words came out scrambled, so I knelt instead
and prayed in the chapel of Motherhood, prayed
for that whole wild fucking queendom,
its sorrow, its unbearable skinless beauty,
and all the souls that were in it. I prayed and prayed
until my voice was a nightcry
and sunlight pixelated my face like a kaleidoscope.

Sujata Bhatt

Poppies in Translation

for Ioana Ieronim

You tell us how in Romanian,
the wild poppies growing everywhere
are *a living flame of love* –

I imagine a single flame, and then a wildfire
by the roads, in the fields,
even between the railway tracks
where the sun spills through.

Windswept, they might be, these poppies,
    fluttering but confident,
           certain of love and life
as they grow in your poem, in Romanian.

As you speak, I remember those poppies;
as you speak, I imagine their thin, hairy stems
entangled with grass, and can simply feel
the way their wild redness
burns and reels: reckless, reckless with first love –
first sorrow and pain –   I can feel
the way light slides through their skins –
I have seen such poppies.
I have seen crêpe de chine, chiffon,
how their sheerest silks glisten in the sun,
bright as fresh blood.

They could be Hindu brides,
ripening in their red saris,
    as they face Agni –
skin glowing gold on gold on gold.

There are days when the poppies know something more.
Days when even in their restless trembling
          as the wind slaps down,
they ripple with the strength of their ragged petals.

I have seen such poppies:
What you call *a living flame of love*.
Even their stamens, whorls of black filaments,
ache with love – even their anthers,
powdered and smudged bluish black-violet,
                    ache with love.

How else describe their power?

Still, in English, we don't know
          about this love.
Do we dare to say
          their intensity is love?

Who is the speaker in your poem?
Does she have the authority to make such claims?
What is it about your tone, your cadence,
that doesn't carry over into English?
Granted, we accept that *fire* and *flame*
describe more than colour;
granted, we understand strong emotions,
but adding *love* over here, *en passant*,
makes us uneasy.

In English, we say the poppies speak to us,
we say their intensity calls out to us –
and we say it's the urgency
of their *call* that moves us.

Why do we turn them into mouths?
About love we're not certain.
But it could be there, we say.
We can't exclude love,
and yet, we don't want to mention it.
That would be too much:
a living flame of love,
or even, *the intensity of the poppies' love* –
No, we say, no.
But the poppies do call us.

Caroline Bird

Rookie

You thought you could ride a bicycle
but, turns out, those weren't bikes
they were extremely bony horses. And that wasn't
a meal you cooked, that was a microwaved
hockey puck. And that wasn't a book that was
a taco stuffed with daisies. What if
you thought you could tie your laces?
But all this time you were just wrapping
a whole roll of sellotape round your shoe and
hoping for the best? And that piece of paper
you thought was your tax return?
A crayon drawing of a cat. And your best friend
is actually a scarecrow you stole from a field
and carted away in a wheelbarrow.
Your mobile phone is a strip of bark
with numbers scratched into it.
Thousands of people have had to replace
their doors, at much expense, after you
battered theirs to bits with a hammer
believing that was the correct way
to enter a room. You've been pouring pints
over your head. Playing card games with a pack
of stones. Everyone's been so confused
by you: opening a bottle of wine with a cutlass,
lying on the floor of buses, talking to
babies in a terrifyingly loud voice.
All the while nodding to yourself like
'Yeah, this is how it's done.'
Planting daffodils in a bucket of milk.

Malika Booker

The Little Miracles

after 'A Winter Night' by Tomas Tranströmer
(translated by Robin Robertson)

Since I found mother collapsed on the kitchen
floor, we siblings have become blindfolded mules

harnessed to carts filled with strain, lumbering
through a relentless storm, wanting to make

our mother walk on her own again, wanting to rest
our palms on her left leg and arm like Jesus, but

constellations do not gather like leaves in a teacup,
so what miracle, of what blood, of what feeble wishes

do we pray, happy no nails hammer plywood, building
a coffin, to house her dead weight, happy her journey

crawls as we her children hold on like drought holds out
for rain, learning what it is like to begin again, start

with the, the, the dog, the cat, the date, the year, the
stroke, the brain, the fenced in walls, she struggles

to dismantle brick on brick. *She cannot break this*,
we reason, watching her left hand in her lap, a useless

echo. We chew bitter bush, swallow our howling storm,
reluctantly splintering under the strain of our mother's

ailing bed-rest. We smile at each of her feats: right hand
brushing her teeth in late evening, head able to lift

without the aid of a neck-brace, her offspring's names
Malika, Phillip and Kwesi are chants repeated over

and over as if staking us children as her life's work,
her blessings, showing how much we are loved. The days

she sings *walk with me oh my Lord*, over and over, *walk
with me oh my Lord, through the darkest night*... and I sing

with her, my tones flat to her soprano, *just as you changed
the wind and walked upon the sea, conquer, my living Lord,*

the storm that threatens me, and we sing and sing until
she says, *Maliks, please stop the cat-wailing before*

*you voice mek rain fall, and look how the weather nice
outside eh!* Then we laugh and laugh until almost giddy,

our mood light momentarily in this sterile room, where
each spoonful of pureed food slipped into her mouth

like a tender offering takes us a step away from feeding
tubes, and we are so thankful for each minuscule miracle.

Sean Borodale

10th February: Queen

I keep the queen, she is long in my hand,
her legs slightly pliant;
folded, dropped down, wings flat
that flew her mating flight
to the sun and back, full of spermatozoa, dronesong.
She was made mechanically ecstatic.
I magnify what she is, magnify her skews and centres.
How downy she is, fur like a fox's greyness, like a thistle's mane.
Wings perfect, abdomen subtle in shades of brittle;
her rear legs are big in the lens;
feet like hung anchors are hooks for staying on cell-rims.
Veins in her wings are a rootwork of rivers,
all echo and interlace. This is her face, compound eye.
I look at the slope of her head, the mouth's proboscis;
her thin tongue piercing is pink as cut flesh, flash glass.
Some hairs feather and split below the head.
Those eyes are like castanets, cast nets;
woman all feral and ironwork, I slip
under the framework, into the subtle.
The wing is jointed at the black leather shoulder.
I wear it, I am soft to stroke, the lower blade fans.
Third generation queen of our stock,
you fall as I turn. I hold your hunchback;
a carcase of lightness, no grief, part animal, part flower.

Colette Bryce

Derry

I was born between the Creggan and the Bogside
    to the sounds of crowds and smashing glass,
by the river Foyle with its suicides and rip tides.
    I thought that city was nothing less

than the whole and rain-domed universe.
    A teacher's daughter, I was one of nine
faces afloat in the looking-glass
    fixed in the hall, but which was mine?

I wasn't ever sure.
    We walked to school, linked hand in hand
in twos and threes like paper dolls.
    I slowly grew to understand

the way the grey Cathedral cast
    its shadow on our learning, cool,
as sunlight crept from east to west.
    The adult world had tumbled into hell

from where it wouldn't find its way
    for thirty years. The local priest
played Elvis tunes and made us pray
    for starving children, and for peace,

and lastly for 'The King'. At mass we'd chant
    hypnotically, *Hail Holy Queen,*
mother of mercy; sing to Saint
    Columba of his *Small oak grove, O Derry mine.*

*

We'd cross the border in our red Cortina,
    stopped at the checkpoint just too long
for fractious children, searched by a teenager
    drowned in a uniform, cumbered with a gun,

who seemed to think we were trouble-on-the-run
    and not the Von Trapp Family Singers
harmonizing every song
    in rounds to pass the journey quicker.

Smoke coiled up from terraces
    and fog meandered softly down the valley
to the Brandywell and the greyhound races,
    the ancient walls with their huge graffiti,

arms that encircled the old city
    solidly. Beyond their pale,
the Rossville flats – mad vision of modernity;
    snarling crossbreeds leashed to rails.

A robot under remote control like us
    commenced its slow acceleration
towards a device at number six,
    home of the moderate politician;

only a hoax, for once, some boys
    had made from parcel tape and batteries
gathered on forays to the BSR,
    the disused electronics factory.

*

The year was nineteen eighty-one,
    the reign of Thatcher. 'Under Pressure'
was the song that played from pub to pub
    where talk was all of hunger strikers

in the Maze, our jail within a jail.
    A billboard near Free Derry Corner
clocked the days to the funerals
    as riots blazed in the city centre.

Each day, we left for the grammar school,
    behaved ourselves, pulled up our socks
for benevolent Sister Emmanuel
    and the Order of Mercy. Then we'd flock

to the fleet of buses that ferried us
    back to our lives, the Guildhall Square
where Shena Burns our scapegoat drunk
    swayed in her chains like a dancing bear.

On the couch, we cheered as an Irish man
    bid for the Worldwide Featherweight title
and I saw blue bruises on my mother's arms
    when her sleeve fell back while filling the kettle

for tea. My bed against the door,
    I pushed the music up as loud
as it would go and curled up on the floor
    to shut the angry voices out.

*

My candle flame faltered in a cup;
    we were stood outside the barracks in a line
chanting in rhythm, calling for a stop
    to strip searches for the Armagh women.

The proof that Jesus was a Derry man?
    Thirty-three, unemployed and living with his mother,
the old joke ran. While half the town
    were queuing at the broo, the fortunate others

bent to the task of typing out the cheques.
   Boom! We'd jump at another explosion,
windows buckling in their frames, and next
   you could view the smouldering omission

in a row of shops, the missing tooth
   in a street. Gerry Adams' mouth
was out of sync in the goldfish bowl
   of the TV screen, our dubious link

with the world. Each summer, one by one,
   my sisters upped and crossed the water,
armed with a grant from the government
   – the Butler system's final flowers –

until my own turn came about:
   I watched that place grow small before
the plane ascended through the cloud
   and I could not see it clearly any more.

John Burnside

On the Vanishing of My Sister, Aged 3, 1965

They saw her last in our garden of stones and willows.
A few bright twigs and pebbles glazed with rain
and, here and there, amidst the dirt and gravel,
a slick of leaf and milkstone, beautiful
for one long moment in the changing light.
Then she was gone.
My mother had looked away
for a matter of seconds
– she said this, over and over,
as if its logic could undo
the wildness of a universe that stayed
predictable for years, then carried off
a youngest daughter;
my father was in the room at the back of our prefab,
watching the new TV, the announcer
excited, Gold Cup Day
and Arkle romping home by twenty lengths.
Maybe we have to look back, to see
that we have all the makings of bliss – the first spring light,
the trees along the farm road
thick with song;
and surely it was this
that drew her out
to walk into the big
wide world, astonished, suddenly at home
no matter where she was.
It seems, when they found her,
she wasn't the least bit scared.
An hour passed, then another;
my mother waited, while our friends and neighbours
came and went, my father running out
to search, then back again,
taking her, once, in his arms, and trying

vainly to reassure her,
she in her apron,
dusted with icing and flour,
and he too self-contained, too rudely male,
more awkward, now, than when he knew her first:
a marriage come between them, all those years
of good intent
and blithe misunderstanding.
It was Tom Dow who brought her home,
tears in his eyes, the boy we had always known
as the local bully, suddenly finding himself
heroic,
and when they brought her in
and sat her down,
we gathered to stand
in the light of her, life and death
inscribed in the blue of her eyes, and the sweet
confusion of rescue, never having been
endangered.
She's married now, and Tom is married too,
and I, like my father, strayed into
discontent,
not being what was wanted, strange to myself
and wishing, all the time,
that I was lost,
out at the end of winter, turning away
to where the dark begins, far in the trees,
darkness and recent cold and the sense of another
far in the trees, where no one pretends
I belong.

Niall Campbell

The Night Watch

It's 1 a.m. and someone's knocking
at sleep's old, battered door – and who
could it be but this boy I love,
calling for me to come out, into
the buckthorn field of being awake –

and so I go, finding him there
no longer talking – but now crying
and crying, wanting to be held;
but *shhh*, what did you want to show
that couldn't wait until the morning?

Was it the moon – because I see it:
the first good bead on a one-bead string;
was it the quiet – because I owned it,
once – but found I wanted more.

Vahni Capildeo

Investigation of Past Shoes

INSIDE THE GATEWAY: 1970S RED CLOGS WITH SIDE BUCKLE

The forever shoe, which points homewards, belongs to my mother. When our house was being built, she stepped onto the driveway while the tarmac was still wet, still setting. Ever since that step, the driveway, which slants upwards, bears an imprint of her 1971 footwear. Her footprint says, *Climb! Come with me.* Whoever steps into that impression becomes, for a moment, the leggy wearer of a fire-red clog with a piratical silver buckle on the side.

OUTSIDE THE TEMPLE: GOLD AND SILVER SANDALS

The sandals which will make a female of me belong to many women. The front of the temple entrance hides itself behind shoe-racks. Visitors enter barefooted, leaving behind the dung, dried frogs, spilled petrol and ketchup traces of the streets. Hundreds of pairs of gold and silver sandals wait here for the women who will re-emerge from the vigil with the taste of basil leaf and sugar in their deep-breathing mouths and carpet fibres between their toes. The sandals, gold and silver, seem all alike. How can the women tell them apart? They do tell them apart. It is as if each pair sings an intimate mantra to its owner, audible only to her. One day I too shall return to expectant slippers that stack up like the moon and the stars outside a marble building; one day I shall not have to wear child's shoes.

SUNDAY BEFORE SCHOOL: WHITE SNEAKERS

Seven years of these shoes are a chemical memory. The Convent ruled that pupils' shoes must be white: absolutely white. Who can imagine a 1980s shoe that was absolutely white, without any logo, with no swoosh, not a single slogan? Sunday evenings, before the school week,

I crouched down on the pink bathroom tiles and painted my shoes into the absolute of whiteness; like the Alice in Wonderland gardeners repainting roses. This task was performed with a toothbrush and with special paste that annihilated so many design features. Purity was attained by the application of a whitener that stank of scientific polysyllables. Convent-girl identity. Tabula rasa. Toxicity and intoxication: with good intentions, getting high on paste.

BAD MARRIAGE SHOES: SILVER BALLET SLIPPERS

When I met my ex, I was already committed to heels: black ankle boots with four-inch stacks for walking through snow; French cream curved suede stilettos for scaling fire-escape ladders on to rooftops to admire the winter sky; even after I left him, scarlet satin bedroom-only spiky mules to amuse myself. Early on, my ex said that the way women walk in heels looks ugly. And my nails made unnatural social appearances: emerald lacquer; cobalt; incarnadine. Sign of a bad marriage: I began to wear flats. The penitential mermaid shoes, worn once and once only, were a Gabor creation: distressed silver ballet slippers with netted and criss-cross side details which would make the material seem to swish with the changes of light on feet that go walking. Cool as moonlight on a tourist coastline. But the inner stitching hooked the softness of my skin which has always been too soft; but I could not turn back, for we had tickets to an evening of Mozart; but the paper tissues that I stuffed into my shoes failed to act as a protective lining. Paper tissue snow-flecks teardropped with crimson blood created a trail behind me as I ascended the many tiers of the wedding-cake concert hall.

BAREFOOT: PEARL PINK POLISH

Sitting next to someone can make my feet curl: shy, self-destructive and oyster-like, they want to shuck their cases, to present themselves, little undersea pinks; their skin still is too soft, their toes still too long, their ankles still too slender, for a modern fit. But he is not modern; he sits like stone, and my bare feet are cool, they will not have to bleed.

Mary Jean Chan

The Window

after Marie Howe

Once in a lifetime, you will gesture
at an open window, tell the one who
detests the queerness in you that dead
daughters do not disappoint, free your
sore knees from inching towards a kind
of reprieve, declare yourself genderless
as hawk or sparrow: an encumbered body
let loose from its cage. You will refuse
your mother's rage, her spit, her tongue
heavy like the heaviest of stones. Her
anger is like the sun, which is like love,
which is the easiest thing, even on the
hardest of days. You will linger, knowing
that this standing before an open window
is what the living do: that they sometimes
reconsider at the slightest touch of grace.

Brendan Cleary

It's Our Dance

for Lorna

Every Sunday
I play Nina Simone's
'My baby just cares for me'
& with a different flower
in your hair every week
you spring out from the bar
& I leave the mixing desk
& we dance with our hangovers,
yes we dance around the bar
& last week we ended up
outside briefly on Lewes Road
in the petrol hazes
& we even waltzed
out to the beer garden
& everybody smiles
when we dance together
to 'My baby just cares for me'
& for a few precious minutes
it's as if we have all swallowed the moon
& everyone is lighter
& the world might not ever end.

Loretta Collins Klobah

Peckham, London, Cold Water Flat

The last bus brings our men home from the night kitchens
while we feed her baby rice and Tabasco;
tie baby on the back with an African wrap,
and she sleeps. We watch British comedies
about bothersome, faded women, on the tele.
We break French and English trying
make sense of our lives, create our private pidgin.
On Saturdays we count coins, stroll Brixton market
to pick out yam, pepper, tomato, and a scrap of fish.
I buy pirate recordings of Stone Love Sound Clash.
When I'm leaving for good, going back to the Caribbean,
she brings me to her bedroom, where she unpacks *pagnes*
from home, Dutch Waxes, printed with flying fish
and stingray, and one green dress, fabric sheeny
with moon and star pattern when sun and shadow catches it.
Handpainted yellow cogs of colour wheel around the skirt;
uneven yellow rickrack adorns the neck.
A dress stitched in her Cote D'Ivoire. I will wear it
until the green fades to grey and patches of my skin
shine through thinning cloth. She brings out a pair
of embroidered satin high heels from Paris, impossibly
large for her feet or mine. She shows me how
she places paper in the toe to keep them in place.
I slide my feet in and try to raise myself
to that elevation. Feel the pinch of the paper.
Did she wear these shoes? They are beautiful.
The wadded paper, the way she helps me
hobble across the room to the mirror make them beautiful.
I will never wear them, but I place them in my bag,
promise to send American jeans and the hottest salsa music.
During the days, I have visited Notting Hill Carnival camps,
learned to play pan and sew parrot feathers, reasoned
with calypsonian Lord Cloak, drunk Carib with the sound-

lorry men and the women sewing spangles on spandex,
and interviewed a borough councillor who complained that
those West Indian riot-muckers pissed in his yard
and got too political with Carnival floats about Apartheid,
which went "like a swarm of bees" down the road.
At night, we have waited up together, both shy –
I, a guest in her home, a tramp picked up by her boarder
at an Africa Centre dance – grateful for a cold water flat
and kind lover to keep me warm. Her husband and my man, chefs,
work graveyard shifts and then ride the long night bus to Peckham.
Later, long after my good man goes off with an Italian gal
and I also travel to new, sadder romantic destinations,
the female friendship, of course, remains.
We exchange yearly photos of our daughters now and cards.
The yellow cogs on my worn-out green dress resemble
steel pan heads – I wear the music of London.
And I think of her and her warm cold water home.

David Constantine

The Rec

Back home and finding the rec gone
Flogged off, become a gated community
CCTV in every hanging basket
And identical shaven-headed fat men
Aiming remotes each at his own portcullis

How can I make of it a 'luminous emptiness'
As Heaney did of his axed chestnut tree?
It's a space stuffed full with hardware
Loungers and meat. At thirty paces
It lights up sodium white. Pitbulls prowl the wire.

Oh that man who stands at the bus-stop all day long
And whatever number bus comes he never gets on
But tells everybody waiting, It was all fields round here
When I was a boy – day by day, more and more
He's me. I tell them Miss Eliza Smythe left the rec

In trust to the Town in perpetuity
For the health of children, her line dying out.
It was an old enclosure quick-set with hawthorn
And we lay there watching and waiting for our turn
In a team-game on the free ground under the open sky.

Only the moon and stars lit up the rec.
Few still believe there was such a playing-place
But, yes, another elegy would be very nice
So remember all you like. Can we live on lack?
Should have stopped them grabbing it. Should take it back.

Robert Crawford

Herakleitos

eftir Kallimachos

Herakleitos,
Whan they telt me
Ye'd deed
Wey bak,
I grat,
Mindin
Yon nicht
We sat oot gabbing
Till the cauld
Peep o day.
An sae, ma auld
Halikarnassian pal,
Ye got seik
And noo ye're someplace
Deid in the grun –
But thae sangs, aa
Yon nichtingales o yourn,
Still soun
Lik they sounded
Then
When we set oot
An sat oot,
Twa young men.
Daith taks the lot,
They sey,
But, ach,
Thae sangs
He's nivver
Gonnae get.

in memory of Mick Imlah
telt told; *deed* died; *grat* wept; *gabbing* talking; *peep o day* dawn; *seik*
ill; *grun* ground; *yourn* yours; *soun* sound

Emily Critchley

Something wonderful has happened it is called you

And mostly these days I just like to look
at you and sometimes make words
out of your name or rock you
in my arms till the thought of I
with or without poetry
no longer matters.
It's not like I have forgotten
how to worry

    – the disappearing forests
      vanishing species
      zone of sky above our heads –

I pray that when you are older there may still be
the forests, for instance, and the species

    – precious zone of sky
      to keep sun off yr precious face –

And not just in the zoo.
I worry about other things too but mostly
it is hard to be unhappy these days
especially now the spring's advancing
and you're learning
about hands, how to hold things in them
and take everything it's yours.

Nichola Deane

Yesterday's Child

Sorrow and rage, rage and sorrow
are beads on a thread of ragged prayer

and yesterday's child can't cut the string
and her life is strung on thin thin air

she ever doggedly sowing tomorrow
with sorrow and rage and rage and sorrow

Tishani Doshi

Girls Are Coming Out of the Woods

for Monika

Girls are coming out of the woods,
wrapped in cloaks and hoods,
carrying iron bars and candles
and a multitude of scars, collected
on acres of premature grass and city
buses, in temples and bars. Girls
are coming out of the woods
with panties tied around their lips,
making such a noise, it's impossible
to hear. Is the world speaking too?
Is it really asking, *What does it mean
to give someone a proper resting?* Girls are
coming out of the woods, lifting
their broken legs high, leaking secrets
from unfastened thighs, all the lies
whispered by strangers and swimming
coaches, and uncles, especially uncles,
who said spreading would be light
and easy, who put bullets in their chests
and fed their pretty faces to fire,
who sucked the mud clean
            off their ribs, and decorated
their coffins with briar. Girls are coming
out of the woods, clearing the ground
to scatter their stories. Even those girls
found naked in ditches and wells,
those forgotten in neglected attics,
and buried in river beds like sediments
from a different century. They've crawled
their way out from behind curtains
of childhood, the silver-pink weight

of their bodies pushing against water,
against the sad, feathered tarnish
of remembrance. Girls are coming out
of the woods the way birds arrive
at morning windows – pecking
and humming, until all you can hear
is the smash of their minuscule hearts
against glass, the bright desperation
of sound – bashing, disappearing.
Girls are coming out of the woods.
They're coming. They're coming.

Sarah Doyle

The woman who married an alchemist

He chose me for my dullness, he told me; the challenge
of it, of replacing my sickly patina with glow. *I know
a project when I see one*, he said, appraising the weight
on me, the soft lead bulk that settled round my bones.
He set to work, stoking fires and sweltering at phials,

pinching my skin between his thumb and forefinger,
a fever of text coiling from his lips. He stroked
my breasts, my belly, my hips with a practised hand,
though never with a man's desire; I was metallurgy,
and no match for his iron resolve. Those first weeks,

my blood fizzed with heat and my pores secreted a
sulphurous odour whose rotting breath choked the air
around me. He was mercurial: shrill with triumph
at every slight yellowing, bitter with recriminations
when the grey of my tarnish bloomed once more.

He dowsed me with water, kindled flames at my feet,
packed me in salt. It was my fault, I was never more
than alloy, a bastard mix that was temporary at best.
He radiated ire, raged that I had the brass neck to stand
there, useless as pyrite, fool that I was. He considered

veneering my skin with gilt, but would always feel
the difference, he said; how my lustre was superficial,
lacking the subcutaneous value he craved. I willed
myself to shine for him, but was made of baser stuff.
Never golden. Never precious. Never good enough.

Nick Drake

Through the Red Light

I saw him at rush hour, courier
appearing from the primordial chaos
of the underpass into the dawn array's
thousand windscreens mirroring the sun,

on the spooky geometry of his racing bike,
cans clamped to his head, ticks on his heels,
stubble glitter-gold on his cool face,
not giving a flying fuck about red lights –

As he scanned me sideways with a passing
glance I swear I caught a shock of light,
a handful of sparks, wild fire in the pixelated
secret of his eyes – then the red turned green

but he was out of range, zigzag
zooming away as everyone gave chase

Carol Ann Duffy

Empty Nest

Dear child, the house pines when you leave.
I research whether there is any bird who grieves
over its empty nest.

                Your vacant room
is a still-life framed by the unclosed door;
read by sunlight, an open book on the floor.

I fold the laundry; hang your flower dress
in darkness. Forget-me-nots.

*

Beyond the tall fence, I hear horse-chestnuts
counting themselves.
                    Then autumn; Christmas.
You come and go, singing. Then ice; snowdrops.

Our home hides its face in hands of silence.

I knew mothering, but not this other thing
which hefts my heart each day. Heavier.
Now I know.

*

This is the shy sorrow. It will not speak up.
I play one chord on the piano;
                          it vanishes, tactful,
as dusk muffles the garden; a magpie staring from its branch.
The marble girl standing by the bench.

From the local church, bells like a spelling.
And the evening star like a text.
And then what next...

Ian Duhig

Bridled Vows

I will be faithful to you, I do vow,
but not until the seas have all run dry
et cetera. Although I mean it now
I'm not a prophet and I will not lie.

To be your perfect wife, I could not swear;
I'll love, yes; honour (maybe); won't obey,
but will co-operate if you will care
as much as you are seeming to today.

I'll do my best to be your better half,
but I don't have the patience of a saint
and at you, not with you, I'll sometimes laugh,
and snap too, though I'll try to show restraint.

We might work out. No blame if we do not.
With all my heart, I think it's worth a shot.

Kate Edwards

Frequency Violet

Some have misgivings about Violet. They believe
she is on the spectrum; somewhere at the very end,
in fact. None can account for it but we're told
she hums inaudibly in the octave of ozone, and lives
in an airlock, loiters in restricted zones, makes
uncanny utterances, keeps marine snails, crushes
pencils into graphite dust, dances like it's the seventies,
tattoos the world's conspiracy theories onto uterine vellum,
stays up all night smoothing polymers under strip lights,
blinking. Rumours insist she has an eye for tactical missile
design and stockpiles blueprints, knows how to execute
the perfect gem heist and leave fingerprints all over it.
Her party trick will make volatile hearts and auras
of loneliness glow in the dark; despondency shine black.
Dreams of Violet often precede a wedding or a gas attack.

Rhian Edwards

Skype

for B.L.H.

Now we have fallen by way
of a window, the motion
picture of a mouth, the faithful
companion of the voice,
staggered by a split
second.

Now we can only see the other
by looking away from the lens,
the voyeur conversing
conversing with its prey,
caressing your face
with a cursor.

Now we have come to a blur,
a pixelated mashing of atoms,
stock-stilled in vignette,
we re-focus the cynosure
with the fractious waking
of a bleary eye.

Now we are a screen, a sea
apart. Three thousand miles
as the crow flies, you lean
in for the kiss with only
the blue iris of the camera
to requite it.

Helen Farish

A Night in at Nohant

*(One player shuffles a pack of homemade cards, picks a musical key;
the player opposite must describe the key using words or phrases.
Advanced players only: keys can be replaced with single notes.)*

A minor – rain, mansard roofs,
the heart a bedraggled stray animal
looking at the turning of wheels,
the silk button you recall
your mother stitching onto the pleat
of a blue coat with grey lining.

C major – blocks of colour: the sea,
a field, kittens, a child, a daffodil.

E flat major – white china plates,
to be the last of a party on its way
to the river, the seed-heavy heads
of grasses brushed by skirts, notes
like butter left in a warm dish.

B – on a faded wall of thin-sky blue, the trembling
reflection of the smallest pane in the house,
the late low sun netted in a mesh of leaves.

F sharp – snow-melt filling the grooves
of carriage wheels as you walk along
rue Rivoli at dusk; the moss which spends
its winter covering the arm of a stone seat;
that woman you remember shaking a red rug
from the first floor window of a white house
in a city you've forgotten or confuse.

Paul Farley

The Power

Forget all of that end-of-the-pier
palm-reading stuff. Picture a seaside town
in your head. Start from its salt-wrack-rotten smells
and raise the lid of the world to change the light,
then go as far as you want: the ornament
of a promenade, the brilliant greys of gulls,
the weak grip of a crane in the arcades
you've built, ballrooms to come alive at night,
then a million-starling roost, an opulent
crumbling like cake icing...
                            Now, bring it down
in the kind of fire that flows along ceilings,
that knows the spectral blues; that always starts
in donut fryers or boardwalk kindling
in the dead hour before dawn, that leaves pilings
marooned by mindless tides, that sends a plume
of black smoke high enough to stain the halls
of clouds. Now look around your tiny room
and tell me that you haven't got the power.

Parwana Fayyaz

Forty Names

I

Zib was young.
Her youth was all she cared for.
These mountains were her cots
The wind her wings, and those pebbles were her friends.
Their clay hut, a hut for all the eight women,
And her father, a shepherd.

He knew every cave and all possible ponds.
He took her to herd with him,
As the youngest daughter
Zib marched with her father.
She learnt the ways to the caves and the ponds.

Young women gathered there for water, the young
Girls with the bright dresses, their green
Eyes were the muses.

Behind those mountains
She dug a deep hole,
Storing a pile of pebbles.

II

The daffodils
Never grew here before,
But what is this yellow sea up high on the hills?

A line of some blue wildflowers.
In a lane toward the pile of tumbleweeds
All the houses for the cicadas,

All your neighbors.
And the eagle roars in the distance,
Have you met them yet?

The sky above through the opaque skin of
Your dust carries whims from the mountains,
It brings me a story.
The story of forty young bodies.

III

A knock,
Father opened the door,
There stood the fathers,
The mothers' faces startled.
All the daughters standing behind them
In the pit of dark night,
Their yellow and turquoise colors
Lining the sky.

'Zibon, my daughter,
Take them to the cave.'
She was handed a lantern.
She took the way,
Behind her a herd of colors flowing.
The night was slow,
The sound of their footsteps a solo music of a mystic.

Names:
Sediqa, Hakima, Roqia,
Firoza, Lilia, and Soghra.
Shah Bakhat, Shah Dokht, Zamaroot,
Nazanin, Gul Badan, Fatima, and Fariba.
Sharifa, Marifa, Zinab, Fakhria, Shahparak, MahGol,
Latifa, Shukria, Khadija, Taj Begum, Kubra, Yaqoot,
Fatima, Zahra, Yaqoot, Khadija, Taj, Gol, Mahrokh, Nigina,

Maryam, Zarin, Zara, Zari, Zamin,
Zarina,

At last Zibon.

IV

No news. Neither drums nor flutes of
Shepherds reached them, they
Remained in the cave. Were
People gone?

Once in every night, an exhausting
Tear dropped – heard from someone's mouth,
A whim. A total silence again

Zib calmed them. Each daughter
Crawled under her veil,
Slowly the last throbs from the mill house

Also died.
No throbbing. No pond. No nights.
Silence became an exhausting noise.

V

Zib led the daughters to the mountains.

The view of the thrashing horses, the brown uniforms
All puzzled them. Imagined
The men snatching their skirts, they feared.

We will all meet in paradise,
With our honored faces
Angels will greet us.

A wave of colors dived behind the mountains,
Freedom was sought in their veils, their colors
Flew with wind. Their bodies freed and slowly hit

The mountains. One by one, they rested. Women
Figures covered the other side of the mountains,
Hairs tugged. Heads stilled. Their arms curved
Beside their twisted legs.

These mountains became their cots
The wind their wings, and those pebbles their friends.
Their rocky cave, a cave for all the forty women,
And their fathers and mothers disappeared.

Vicki Feaver

The Larder

Yesterday it was the blaze
of a broom bush; the day before

the peppermint whiff
of a beeswax lip-balm.

Each day, I fill the shelves
with things to remember.

Today, it's the powdery bloom
on the skin of a blueberry,

turning it, cold from the fridge,
between my thumb and finger;

noticing the petal-shaped crater
where the flower withered

and the small hole
where it was pulled

from the stalk; crushing
its tangy pulp on my tongue.

Leontia Flynn

The Radio

The radio hoots and mutters, hoots and mutters
out of the dark, each morning of my childhood.
A kind of plaintive, reedy, oboe note –
Deadlock … it mutters, *firearms* … *Sunningdale*;
Just before two this morning … talks between …

and through its aperture, the outside world
comes streaming, like a magic lantern show,
into our bewildered solitude.
Unrest … it hoots now *both sides … sources say …*
My mother stands, like a sentinel, by the sink.

*

I should probably tell you more about my mother:
Sixth child of twelve surviving – 'escapee'
from the half-ignited *powder keg* of Belfast;
from its *escalation*, its *tensions ratcheting*
its *fear of reprisals*, and its *tit-for-tat*.

She is small, freaked out, pragmatic, vigilant;
she's high-pitched and steely – like, in human form,
the RKO transmitter tower, glimpsed
just before films on Sunday afternoons,
where we loaf on poufs – or wet bank holidays.

Or perhaps a strangely tiny lightning rod
snatching the high and wild and worrying words
out of the air, then running them to ground.
My mother sighs and glances briefly round
at her five small children. *How* does she have five kids?

*

Since my mother fell on the Wheel Of Motherhood
– that drags her, gasping, out of bed each dawn
bound to its form – she's had to rally back.
She wrangles her youngsters into one bright room
and tries to resist their centrifugal force

as she tries to resist the harrowing radio,
with its *Diplock* … and *burned out* … and *Disappeared*.
So high, obscure and far from neighbouring farms
is the marvellous bungalow my father built,
birdsong and dog-barks ricochet for miles;

and wasn't my mother wise to stay put here
soothed by the rhythms of a *culchie* Life
– birdsong in chimneys, the Shhhh of coal-truck brakes –
when women at home are queuing round the block
for their '*Valium, thank you doctor, and Librium*'?

*

So daily the radio drops its explosive news
and daily my mother turns to field the blow.
The words fall down, a little neutral now,
onto the stone-cold, cold, stone kitchen floor.
Our boiler slowly digests its anthracite

and somewhere outside, in the navy dark,
my father tends to his herd of unlikely cows.
A *Charolais*, the colour of cement,
thought to be lost for days has just turned up
simply standing – *ta da!*– in front of a concrete wall.

My mother, I think, is like that *Charolais* cow
in the Ulster of 1970 … 80 … what?
with its *tensions* … and its *local sympathies*.
She gets her head down, hidden in plain view,
and keeps us close. '*Look: Nothing to see here – right?*'

But when the night has rolled round again,
my mother will lie unsleeping in her bed;
she'll lie unsleeping in that bungalow bed
and if a car slows on the bend behind the house,
she's up, alert – fearing the worst, which is:

that a child of hers might die – or lose an eye;
or a child *anywhere* die or lose an eye …
That the car which slows on the bend behind the house
– *Midnight* … she thinks now … *random* … *father of five* –
is the agent of vile sectarian attack.

By the top field's wall, our unfenced slurry pit,
(villain of Public Information Films)
widens and gulps beneath the brittle stars.
My mother too thinks the worst, then gulps it back,
and in this way discovers equilibrium.

*

Death in the slurry pit, death beside the curb.
Death on the doorstep, bright-eyed, breathing hard.
My mother folds the tender, wobbling limbs
and outsized heads of her infants into herself;
she curls up, foetal, over our foetal forms.

Since my mother sailed down the Mekong river at nightfall
to the Heart of Darkness that is motherhood,
her mind's been an assemblage of wounds.
She thinks about Gerard McKinney, Jean McConville
– later the eyes of Madeleine McCann

will level their gaze from every pleading poster
and pierce her heart like a rapier – needle-thin
as the high, wild, hardly audible cries of children.

Men of Violence … says the radio.
My mother nods, then finally falls asleep.

    *

And what if after my mother falls asleep
the hoots, half-words, and notes of high alarm
get loose from her head on little soot-soft wings?
Say they flap like bats. They fuck with the carriage clock.
They settle on her Hummel figurines.

Till the whole contraption of that home-made house
creaks, roars and bulges with the soundless strain
of my mother trying not to be afraid …
Forgive me, this is all hypothesis.
It's conjecture, Doctor, of the crudest sort …

Its gist being: beneath our bonhomie
and tight commercial smiles, this tone or timbre
flows on, like a circuit thrown into reverse –
and at the centre of concentric circles
that this is what plays behind an unmarked door.

    *

Sometimes, rather, lying in my bed
I seem to hear the sound of the radio
issuing from a room, deep in the house;
it tells, in mournful tones, how two young men
were *taken from their car beside the road …*

and afterwards … nothing. All the stars come out
like sparkling glitter in a magic globe
that ends beyond the dunes fringing the fields –
and because I'm still a child and understand
nothing at all, I simply fall asleep.

Matthew Francis

Ladybird Summer

That summer there was a plague of ladybirds, drifting
    over the garden in a reddish smoke.
        We'd find them on the carpet,
a smattering of coral beads from a broken necklace,
    but self-willed, crawling every which way, mating
        like tiddlywinks.

The flowering season for insects. Crickets twitched the grass,
    moths trundled under their paper-dart wings
        or crouched on the ceiling
in the circle of brighter light above the lampshade,
    and the mosquitoes balanced on the wall
        on moon-lander legs.

Trees split in the heat. We drove through a tawny country
    now turned to outback. In the pub courtyard
        we talked till the colour
drained from the petunias in the hanging baskets,
    unwilling to go home carrying the weight
        of the day's air.

There was too much summer. The ladybirds that gathered
    on ledges to be crunched by the closing windows
        had lost their picture-book brightness.
We were glad of the first sign of autumn, a bowl of plums,
    frost blooming on their skin, and tart sunshine
        in their yellow flesh.

Isabel Galleymore

The Starfish

creeps like expired meat –
fizzy-skinned, pentamerously-legged,
her underfur of sucking feet
shivers upon an immobile mussel
whose navy mackintosh is zipped
against the anchor of this fat paw,
this seemingly soft nutcracker who exerts
such pressure until the mussel's jaw
drops a single millimetre. Into this cleft
she'll press the shopping bag of her stomach
and turn the mollusc into broth,
haul in the goods and stumble off,
leaving a vacant cubicle,
a prayer come apart.

Alan Gillis

Bulletin from The Daily Mail

You must have seen those Rent Street potheads,
their skin all sweating processed chicken meat:
knives taped to their thighs, blood-red dots for eyes,
stolen shoes like rocketblasters on their feet?

As sure as rainfall, they're at the entrance to the mall,
tattooed necks livid with love bites.
Hooked to mobile phones, they know your way home
and they wait for you in alleyways at night.

They spit on the bus, their fingers are warty,
they set fire to schools, sniff WD40,
they climb any fence, they climb any roof,
they jump on your bonnet and smash your sunroof,

they'll squeeze through your window and creep up your stairs,
they'll leave your comb crawling with their pubic hairs,
they'll crowbar your gold teeth right out of your head,
they excrete on the street, and they don't go to bed.

Louise Glück

An Adventure

1.

It came to me one night as I was falling asleep
that I had finished with those amorous adventures
to which I had long been a slave. Finished with love?
my heart murmured. To which I responded that many profound
  discoveries
awaited us, hoping, at the same time, I would not be asked
to name them. For I could not name them. But the belief that they
  existed –
surely this counted for something?

2.

The next night brought the same thought,
this time concerning poetry, and in the nights that followed
various other passions and sensations were, in the same way,
set aside forever, and each night my heart
protested its future, like a small child being deprived of a favorite toy.
But these farewells, I said, are the way of things.
And once more I alluded to the vast territory
opening to us with each valediction. And with that phrase I became
a glorious knight riding into the setting sun, and my heart
became the steed underneath me.

3.

I was, you will understand, entering the kingdom of death,
though why this landscape was so conventional
I could not say. Here, too, the days were very long
while the years were very short. The sun sank over the far mountain.
The stars shone, the moon waxed and waned. Soon
faces from the past appeared to me:
my mother and father, my infant sister; they had not, it seemed,
finished what they had to say, though now
I could hear them because my heart was still.

4.

At this point, I attained the precipice
but the trail did not, I saw, descend on the other side;
rather, having flattened out, it continued at this altitude
as far as the eye could see, though gradually
the mountain that supported it completely dissolved
so that I found myself riding steadily through the air –
All around, the dead were cheering me on, the joy of finding them
obliterated by the task of responding to them –

5.

As we had all been flesh together,
now we were mist.
As we had been before objects with shadows,
now we were substance without form, like evaporated chemicals.
Neigh, neigh, said my heart,
or perhaps nay, nay – it was hard to know.

6.

Here the vision ended. I was in my bed, the morning sun
contentedly rising, the feather comforter
mounded in white drifts over my lower body.
You had been with me –
there was a dent in the second pillow case.
We had escaped from death –
or was this the view from the precipice?

Rebecca Goss

Stretch Marks

My swims kept those scars at bay,
two thousand lengths it took, to form

my mapless globe. No trace she was here,
her travels around me refused to surface

as she dived between poles, lapped
that black belly ocean. Once born, meridian

of my achievements, she went off course.
I followed her divergent route, but this was not

her geography. I have wished for them,
a record of her tracks, all snowed over, gone.

Jorie Graham

Tree

Today on two legs stood and reached to the right spot as I saw it
choosing among the twisting branches and multifaceted changing
    shades,
and greens, and shades of greens, lobed, and lashing sun, the fig
    that seemed to me the
perfect one, the ready one, it is permitted, it is possible, it is

actual. The VR glasses are not needed yet, not for now, no, not
    for this while
longer. And it is warm in my cupped palm. And my fingers close
    round but not too
fast. Somewhere wind like a hammerstroke slows down and
    lengthens
endlessly. Closer-in the bird whose coin-toss on a metal tray never
    stills to one

face. Something is preparing to begin again. It is not us. *Shhh* say
    the spreading sails of
cicadas as the winch of noon takes hold and we are wrapped in day
    and hoisted
up, all the ribs of time showing through in the growing in the
    lengthening
harness of sound – some gnats nearby, a fly where the white
    milk-drop

of the torn stem starts. Dust on the eglantine skin, white powder
    in the confetti of light
all up the branches, truth, sweetness of blood-scent and hauled-in
    light, withers of
the wild carnival of tree shaking once as the fruit is removed from
    its dream. Remain I
think backing away from the trembling into full corrosive sun.
    Momentary blindness

follows. Correction. There are only moments. They hurt.
    Correction. Must I put down
here that this is long ago. That the sky has been invisible for
    years now. That the ash
of our fires has covered the sun. That the fruit is stunted yellow
    mould when it appears
at all and we have no produce to speak of. No longer exists. All
    my attention is

free for you to use. I can cast farther and farther out, before the
    change, a page turned,
we have gone into another story, history floundered or one day
    the birds dis-
appeared. The imagination tried to go here when we asked it to,
    from where I hold the
fruit in my right hand, but it would not go. Where is it now.
    Where is this here where

you and I look up trying to make sense of the normal, turn it to
    life, more life,
disinterred from desire, heaved up onto the dry shore awaiting
    the others who could
not join us in the end. For good. I want to walk to the left around
    this tree I have made
again. I want to sit under it full of secrecy insight immensity
    vigour bursting complexity

swarm. Oh great forwards and backwards. I never felt my face
    change into my new
face. Where am I facing now. Is the question of good still
    stinging the open before us
with its muggy destination pitched into nothingness? Something
    expands in you
where it wrenches-up its bright policing into view – is this good,
    is this the good –

under the celebrating crowd, inside the silences it forces hard
  away all round itself,
where chanting thins, where we win the war again, made thin by
  bravery and belief,
here's a polaroid if you want, here's a souvenir, here now for you
  to watch, unfold, up
close, the fruit is opening, the ribs will widen now, it is all seed,
  reddish foam, history.

Lavinia Greenlaw

The break

Deep in the dark of that year
I issued a warning. *I'm going to break*, I said
but quietly and so often that it sounded like a refrain.
People nodded and moved on. What else could they do?
Hold me? Through each and every day?
They had their own days.
One night something paused in the empty street
and tipped me sideways before moving on
and I discovered the pain I'd been trying to speak of.
I was two things now – the shocked engine
and the broken part I carried the last mile home
as if it were something I could then set down.
I met every kindness that followed with astonishment
even when they held up pictures and said
You have every reason to be in such pain.
They had looked inside me and found reasons.
To my mind, these people were gods.
I told my beloved I'd look after myself
but he kept approaching with care and patience
while I issued warnings as a form of encouragement.
There was an instant simplification of our long romance:
we spoke only of pillows, medication, tea and bread.
For months I woke beside my pain
and waited for it to knit itself to me – to become something
I carried without feeling, something incorporated
to the extent that it is not known.
Why, when I had the chance, did I not just set it down?
In what way does it complete me?

Jen Hadfield

Definitions

after Jerome Rothenberg

The Brisket
This cinched consonant, hunched muscle in a yellow
simmet, could also signify a journey. It could feed a family,
or stop the third gob of the three-headed dog. You bind it
to your stick as you set off for the Underworld. Browned, it
melts into punctuated mud, is thick fuel for migrations,
night flights you can't remember. It's a passing madness in
the cat; it makes him a round-eyed bawling bob-cat. It
squirms under the distal phalanges of a splayed hand. It
bucks the bite of the knife. It foams fat.

The Cat
is sleeping very deeply now it's spring been off his head
hunting rabbits all night, in the far-out stones and discoball
eyes of the clifftop crö. His days a kind of stoned remission:
heart-beat irregular, muscles leaping violently in sleep. The
wet bracelet of his mouth unlatched; chattering a little; his
eyelids half-open. His furry buffers nicely spread all about
him; nicely buffered by fat and fur all round.

Equus Primus
as if some god having turned out another batch of
underdone horses (thin as leaves, dappled like leaves) freed
them on the hill to flicker like a thicket of hornbeam and
willow; set down his cutter and balled the waste dough.
Thence this tribe of blackened emoticons, tough as plugs.

The Word 'Died'
It's a cliff-sided stack: sheer, almost an island. A human
can't stand upon that high, tilted pasture but life crowds its
cliffs: sheep and nesting maas, the waste-not plants of
heath and moor. You hear the waves breaking but can't see
them. You shrink down into yourself as you reach the edge:
getting your head around where you are. It's marvellous.
It's aweful. It is always on. Like a massive *and* unfolding its
wings, and mantling. It was here all along, reached by
Shirva and the derelict mills; turf sweating in the hot,
midgy smirr.

The Mackerel
At once, the three hooks chime. The skin is as supple as the
skin on boiled milk and the eye a hard, roundel pane. It is
or it isn't wormy, it tastes of hot blood and earth, tastes of
long-awaited rain, winter lightning and summer thunder.
Heart-throb; mud-coloured; the cooked flesh is tarnish. The
oatmeal crisp. It tastes of steak, it tastes of cream.

The Northern Lights
– but yes, now you pull over – after the headlights, a raw
shifting glare. I've taken them often for a moon behind
cloud. An ambiguous rustling, yes, maybe listening in, when
being overheard is your greatest fear. Like an infection of the
lymph, a shooting-up – that single, white flare.

The Orange
Bloated, swollen with sea-water, it's a boast, fraught with
salt syrup. It forces your fingers apart and makes much of
itself. It is über, *aaber*. A very straining round real orange,
stinking of orange and the sea; stinking of stale cologne.
The sea returns whatever you give it, more so, realler.
Headachy wax! It rolls down the sand into the foam. It
spins at the crest of the breaker!

The Parents
are on the pale brisk longbusy birdbrushed billows of the
equinoctial sea. Without them is a long, unhappy holiday.
Who else gives a shit about your shitty knee? You're
breathless at the thought of them all-night on the sea.
Blithely they step into its bright pale machinery. They
make mandalas of quartz and limpet-shells, hide cash under
a hairbrush, vanish with their luggage as pixies might. The
pillows squared to each other. The sheets pulled tight.

The Pig
is as they say, very human, though our bellies do not
resemble her belly, which is like one of the papyriform
columns at Luxor. Nor can we liken our nipples to her
torment of buttons, our ears to her arums. Our lugs are
unfringed with soft, blonde baleen. But her fetishes: her
forked stick; her devilish loop of rotted rope. Her precious
rasher of chicken wire. Her tired, human eye. Her
constancy as a conspirator.

The Puffballs
Somebody's watching. Two toughened eyeballs propped
behind you on the turf.

The Puffin
A tangled marionette, strings of jerked sinew. Summer's
end, the derelict burrow, a ring of dirty down. An
arabesque of smelly bone, meat for flies and the darling
turf. The head may be full of meat; the large beak, faded: a
Fabergé egg.

The Road to the North Light
It weeps tar from tender parts like frogskin. Thin, mobile
muscles squirm under your soles as it bears you across the
Hill Dyke on a current of cool air, the bed of an invisible
river. It has heather and tormentil, not dandelion but catsear.
It has a creep over a precipice; it has sorrel, parched and tiny.
It carries you above the white and lilac sea; it switchbacks,
and turns you before the sun like a sacrifice.

The Slater
We alone among the creatures are known to imagine our
own minds. Like this woodlouse on the kitchen floor. It
perceives you, rears and comes about. Stroking with its
spurred feet a precipitate of dried soup, a peel hovering
above its own shadow.

The Waxcaps
Someone was carried across this field, bleeding steadily.

Nafeesa Hamid

Doctor's appointment

My mind is all woman. It is uneasy. My doctor tells me part of
my woman is ill. I don't want to woman anymore, I tell him.
He nods without looking at me. His glasses do not budge from
the tip of his nose as he continues to take notes. He asks how
long. I say since my mother birthed me and named me
Woman. He asks how long. I say too long. He says the new
tablets will help me woman again.

Choman Hardi

Dispute Over a Mass Grave

The one you have finished examining
is my son. That is the milky coloured Kurdish
suit his father tailored for him, the blue shirt
his uncle gave to him. Your findings prove
that it is him – he was a tall fifteen year old,
was left handed, had broken a rib.

I know she too has been looking for her son
but you have to tell her that this is not him.
Yes the two of them were playmates and fought
the year before. But it was my son who broke
a rib, hers only feigned to escape trouble.

That one is mine! Please give him back to me.
I will bury him on the verge of my garden –
the mulberry tree will offer him its shadow,
the flowers will earnestly guard his grave,
the hens will peck on his gravestone,
the beehive will hum above his head.

Claire Harman

The Mighty Hudson

'It's odd how they had the same name'
New York Star

After ten years of truck-work, he looked round and sighed:
Left a note for his nephew – 'The parts of my radio' –
And made for the city in a frilled shirt.

Found a walk-up full of the mythical skyline
With the river in front of it grey as a vein
And a tide running up into unreal suburbs.

Practised his weights on a fat co-lodger.
Lifting her one-handed up to the cobwebbed light.
Heard her hot geyser of giggling straight-faced but happy.

Arm-wrestled in bars with less effort than sighing,
Was bought beers by men who pincered his biceps.
Made friends with the barman. Got mystique by not smiling.

Enjoyed a short local career as a hero
After righting a load that got stuck on GW Bridge;
The newspaper posed him lifting a Merc into parking.

Soon after was called by Los Niños Non-Animal Circus
And shot to the top of the bill juggling three girls in lycra;
Their thighs left sequins stuck in his sideburns

And scents that perplexed him: one night he climbed onto their trailer,
Peeled back the roof like a ring-pull,
Picked Leonie out of her bunk through the skylight.

Didn't know his own strength, that's for certain.
Nor hers, when she struck with the whip, with the poker, the shotgun.
The lights of Jersey dimmed in the pith of his head

As he staggered back into the water, his namesake.
Keen as a mother to hurry him home.
Past the dark lighters, the bilge boats:

Past Peekskill, Poughkeepsie and Kingston.
Bear Mountain twirling oddly away like a girl.
The leaves blazing red as the fall, and the branches red too.

Will Harris

SAY

A brick-sized block of grey stone washed ashore on which was carved
the word *SAY*. My dad picked it up at low tide and two months
    later found
another, and another saying *LES*. We worked out that rather than
    a command –
like Rilke's *flow* – it was the name of an old firm, *SAYLES*, which sold
refined sugar, with plantations in the Caribbean and a factory in
    Chiswick.
As capital flows, accumulates and breaks its bounds, so too had
    SAYLES
broken into various subsidiaries. Slipped, dissolved and loosed.
    You find
all kinds of things at low tide. One time, a black retriever came
    wagging up
to me with a jawbone in its mouth. What can't be disposed of
    otherwise –
what can't be broken down – is taken by the river, spat out or lodged

in mud. The SAY brick took pride-of-place on our chest of drawers –
masonry, defaced by time, made part of the furniture. My dad
    decided
to give it to you, in part because you're an artist and he thought it
    looked like
art, but also, which is maybe the same, because it suggested reason
in madness, and made him – made us – less afraid. Last week,
    there was an
acid attack. Two cousins, assumed to be Muslim, having torn off their
clothes, lay naked on the road, calling for help. Passers-by crossed
    the street.
Things break, not flow; it is impossible, however lovely, to see the
    whole

of humanity as a single helix rotating forever in the midst of
    universal time.
Flow, break, flow. That's how things go. Is it? *What are you trying*

to say? After the operation, they stapled shut his stomach. As the scars
healed, it became harder to discuss. He drank as if he had no body
    – nothing
said, admitted to or broken. Flow, break, flow. Gather up the
    fragments.
Now he is back to saying *The country's full. Why are they all men?*
    Four months
ago, in a flimsy hospital gown, the fight had almost left him. In a tone
you'd use to distract a child, the nurse told my mum about her
    holiday to
Sumatra in the early '90s. He likes custard, she replied. We told
    him when
to cough and when to breathe. He clasped a button that controlled
the morphine. Bleep. Bleep. What did the blue and green lines
    mean?
The sudden dips? What was the nurse's name? I chose not to

keep notes. Thoughtful as moss or black coffee, or as the screen of
a dead phone. That's what eyes look like when you really look at
    them.
Inanimate. Moss, though, is alive enough to harvest carbon dioxide,
to grow. Yesterday I googled *thoughtful as moss*, thinking it was from
a Seamus Heaney poem, but only found a description of the poet
"grown long-haired / And thoughtful; a wood-kerne // Escaped
    from
the massacre". At school, we learnt that wood-kernes were armed
peasants who fought against the British in Ireland. I imagined them
(and him) as thoughtful kernels, seeds that had escaped death by
    being
spat out. I am nothing so solid or durable. *What are you trying*

to say? For years I made patterns in the air, not knowing what to say,
then you came and pointed out the paintwork cracked and bubbling
on the wall beside my bed which, though it stank, I hadn't noticed.
The streetlight sparked on beads of damp. Your skin smelt bready,
  warm.
I couldn't say how bare my life had been. The stillness in the room
was like the stillness in the air between the heaves of storm. We
  flowed
into and out of each other, saying – *what?* Saying. Not yet together,
we were incapable of breaking. Cradled in pure being. The paint
  flaked,
exposing streaks of poxy wall. I remembered a church where the
  saints'
faces had been scratched away, taking on a new expression: alien,

afraid. Some days I must look alien to him. Scary. One poet said
the devil was neither *blate nor scaur*, incapable of being scared. I sleep
scared most nights but feel no more holy. Once I pronounced "oven"
often like my mum does, and a friend laughed. The cracks appeared
beneath me. In the years before we met, though I wrote, I was too
  scared –
too scarred – to speak. Flow, flow, flow. I wanted to be carried
  along, not
spat out or upon. That SAY brick picked from the riverbed proved
  that
broken things still flow. *What are you trying to say?* When you asked
me that I closed my laptop, offended. Why? It never mattered what
I said. Whether you speak up or scarcely whisper, you speak with all

you are. To the eye of a being of incomparably longer life – to God
or the devil – the human race would appear as one continuous
  vibration,
in the same way a sparkler twirled at night looks like a circle. In
  darker days

I couldn't say that to my dad, slumped in front of the TV with a mug
of instant coffee. Saying it now only makes me think of times I've
    held
a sparkler – the hiss and flare, the after-smell – which runs counter
to that whole vision. One morning, gagging on his breathing tube,
he started to text my mum, but before he could press send his
    phone
died. He couldn't remember what he tried to say. I can't remember
what I tried to say. Flow, break, flow. You hear me, though?

Seán Hewitt

October

Once, I knelt staring in a garden
in mid-autumn at the last
of the marrow flowers –

a pair pushed up out of nowhere
overnight, too late for the season:
one bent under dew, the frail skin

of the other already turning
slowly back to water.
And yet the leaves bristled

in the wind – the tired petals
not quite ready to give up
to the cold, though each

was a distillation of the sun's
late colour. And I saw myself
kneeling in the garden

from far away, caught between
one man I no longer love,
another I might never.

This is how the world turns:
love like a marrow flower closing,
like another trying still to open.

Selima Hill

The Elephant is Much Too Big to Boogie

The elephant is much too big to boogie
and when I see him standing there like that
he makes me feel very nice and peaceful
like sobbing does when you sob and sob:
so ponderous and dim, he just stands there,
inert not with inertia but with love!
(The elephant is much too big to wink
but when he looks at me he almost does…)

Like summer days when nothing wants to move,
like wardrobes full of sleeping bags, the elephant
has gone to sleep without lying down,
he doesn't need to bother, he's got bones
specially made to double as a bed
for if you want to sleep standing up,
to close your eyes and let enormous planets
roll towards you like delicious buns.

Ellen Hinsey

Evidence THE LAWS

ARTICLE 1.

It is forthwith declared: if by the homeland of their ancestors they are *strangers*—so shall their children be *strangers* too—

ARTICLE 2.

If so identified as *strangers*—they shall no longer be fit to dwell under the common, rough-timbered sky—

ARTICLE 3.

If they labour in the cities, they shall no longer reside in the cities; if they live in the country, they shall be deprived of even the wind-scattered sheaves—

ARTICLE 4.

If thus, they find themselves without labour: *their idleness shall be punishable;*

ARTICLE 5.

And, if the Laws have once pronounced judgment upon them: they shall be forbidden speech in the crowded market square—

ARTICLE 6.

If they find themselves without land, wealth or voice: the *stranger* shall live within the tight confines of the journey—

ARTICLE 7.

Where hours shall be their daily bread and rustic nightfall their only shelter—

ARTICLE 8.

And if, by chance or destiny, a *stranger* should love a *non-stranger*, they too shall be punished—

ARTICLE 9.

Nor shall they benefit from counsel in the white interrogation rooms.

ARTICLE 10.

Where iron hooks shall be roughly affixed to pillars in Justice's basement.

ARTICLE 11.

And although those in attendance shall bear false witness, they will be exempt from forty stripes—

ARTICLE 12.

For no one shall preside over the Laws: *for my beloved, have no doubt—we too are the generation of the Flood.*

Jane Hirshfield

The Supple Deer

The quiet opening
between fence strands
perhaps eighteen inches.

Antlers to hind hooves,
four feet off the ground,
the deer poured through.

No tuft of the coarse white belly hair left behind.

I don't know how a stag turns
into a stream, an arc of water.
I have never felt such accurate envy.

Not of the deer:

To be that porous, to have such largeness pass through me.

Sarah Howe

(c) Tame

'It is more profitable to raise geese than daughters.'
                                    Chinese proverb

This is the tale of the woodsman's daughter. Born with a box
            of ashes set beside the bed,
in case. Before the baby's first cry, he rolled her face into the cinders –
            held it. Weak from the bloom
of too-much-blood, the new mother tried to stop his hand. He dragged
            her out into the yard, flogged her
with the usual branch. If it was magic in the wood, they never
            said, but she began to change:

her scar-ridged back, beneath his lashes, toughened to a rind; it split
            and crusted into bark. Her prone
knees dug in the sandy ground and rooted, questing for water,
            as her work-grained fingers lengthened
into twigs. The tree – a lychee – he continued to curse as if it
            were his wife – its useless, meagre
fruit. Meanwhile the girl survived. Feathered in greyish ash,
            her face tucked in, a little gosling.

He called her Mei Ming: *No Name.* She never learned to speak. Her life
            maimed by her father's sorrow.
For grief is a powerful thing – even for objects never conceived.
            He should have dropped her down
the well. Then at least he could forget. Sometimes when he set
            to work, hefting up his axe
to watch the cleanness of its arc, she butted at his elbow – again,
            again – with her restive head,

till angry, he flapped her from him. But if these silent pleas had
        meaning, neither knew.
The child's only comfort came from nestling under the
        lychee tree. Its shifting branches
whistled her wordless lullabies: the lychees with their watchful eyes,
        the wild geese crossing overhead.
The fruit, the geese. They marked her seasons. She didn't long to join
        the birds, if longing implies

a will beyond the blindest instinct. Then one mid-autumn, she craned
        her neck so far to mark the geese
wheeling through the clouded hills – it kept on stretching – till
        it tapered in a beak. Her pink toes
sprouted webs and claws; her helpless arms found strength
        in wings. The goose daughter
soared to join the arrowed skein: kin linked by a single aim
        and tide, she knew their heading

and their need. They spent that year or more in flight, but where –
        across what sparkling tundral wastes –
I've not heard tell. Some say the fable ended there. But those
        who know the ways of wild geese
know too the obligation to return, to their first dwelling place. Let this
        suffice: late spring. A woodsman
snares a wild goose that spirals clean into his yard – almost like
        it knows. Gripping its sinewed neck

he presses it down into the block, cross-hewn from a lychee trunk.
        A single blow. Profit, loss.

Clive James

Holding Court

Retreating from the world, all I can do
Is build a new world, one demanding less
Acute assessments. Too deaf to keep pace
With conversation, I don't try to guess
At meanings, or unpack a stroke of wit,
But just send silent signals with my face
That claim I've not succumbed to loneliness
And might be ready to come in on cue.
People still turn towards me where I sit.

I used to notice everything, and spoke
A language full of details that I'd seen,
And people were amused; but now I see
Only a little way. What can they mean,
My phrases? They come drifting like the mist
I look through if someone appears to be
Smiling in my direction. Have they been?
This was the time when I most liked to smoke.
My watch-band feels too loose around my wrist.

My body, sensitive in every way
Save one, can still proceed from chair to chair,
But in my mind the fires are dying fast.
Breathe through a scarf. Steer clear of the cold air.
Think less of love and all that you have lost.
You have no future so forget the past.
Let this be no occasion for despair.
Cherish the prison of your waning day.
Remember liberty, and what it cost.

Be pleased that things are simple now, at least,
As certitude succeeds bewilderment.
The storm blew out and this is the dead calm.
The pain is going where the passion went.
Few things will move you now to lose your head
And you can cause, or be caused, little harm.
Tonight you leave your audience content:
You were the ghost they wanted at the feast,
Though none of them recalls a word you said.

Sarah James

Monday, 12th August:
Secrets

       Lies shriek loudest at night,
when Carl sighs   beside me.

3am. Something battles
    against the water pipes.

    The chimney coughs.
     Our fridge's purr turns

  to fierce roar. Claws scrape
on near bricks, the bushes snarl.

     Then a car door slams –
in a stifled metal kiss.

    The walls' muffled thuds,
         shuffling floorboard creakings

and the wind in the rafters
  all hiss 'We know!'

Kathleen Jamie

Blossom

There's this life and no hereafter –
                    I'm sure of that
but still I dither, waiting
for my laggard soul
to leap at the world's touch.

How many May dawns
                    have I slept right through,
the trees courageous with blossom?
Let me number them...

I shall be weighed in the balance
                    and found wanting.
I shall reckon for less
                    than an apple pip.

Jackie Kay

Vault

after Marion Coutts, For the Fallen

And just when we thought, when we thought, when we thought
           We could not   we could not
         We did, we did   we leapt, we leapt
        We made it   across, across.
       We fell often   were broken; we lost.
The past is a leap   in the dark: a dark horse.
         We laughed. We wept. Of course, of course.

Luke Kennard

Crow Baby

Everything plant-delicate. I'm scared to force your arms through
your sleeves. It's like trying to put a little t-shirt on a crow. That's
what it feels like. It feels like I've captured a crow and for some
reason I'm trying to show that crow unconditional love. Only it
keeps pecking me, flapping its wings and flying around the room
and into walls, completely terrified, and I'm like, come on, crow,
don't worry, I'm your father and I love you. Come and perch
on my shoulder. And the crow just flies around the ceiling like
a fan stuck on doublespeed – CAAAAAWWWWW! – stopping
only when it reaches total exhaustion. And then I'm like, I love
you. I love you, crow. I put the crow to my neck and I sit on a
metallic grey exercise ball, the volume right down and subtitles
on because love is so boring. I hum everything my dad used to
play on the piano – stuff I didn't know I remembered. Crow, I
whisper, bouncing ludicrously on the ball, I whisper what I will
whisper five years later, crouched by a drunk man weeping on
Hungerford Bridge, it's going to get better, it's going to get better
and everything is going to be okay.

Mimi Khalvati

The Swarm

Snow was literally swarming round the streetlamp like gnats.
The closer they came, the larger they grew, snow-gnats, snow-bees,

and in my snood, smoking in the snow, I watched them.
Everyone else was behind the door, I could hear their noise

which made the snow, the swarm, more silent. More welcome.
I could have watched for hours and seen nothing more than specks

against the light interrupting light and away from it, flying blind
but carrying light, specks becoming atoms. They flew too fast

to become snow itself, flying in a random panic, looming close
but disappearing, like flakes on the tongue, at the point of recognition.

They died as they landed, riding on their own melting as poems do
and in the morning there was nothing to be seen of them.

Instead, a streak of lemon, lemon honey, ringed the sky
but the cloud-lid never lifted, the weekend promised a blizzard.

I could have watched for hours and seen nothing more than I do now,
an image, metaphor, but not the blind imperative that drove them.

August Kleinzahler

Epistle xxxix

Aggrievius, how is it that I'm certain that you, no other,
will be the one to speak most eloquently at my memorial?
Because it is you, dear friend, who best husbanded
kind remarks of any sort, and, likewise, praise, in life,
the better that it might gush forth now in a single, extravagant go.
There you are, struggling, fighting back your grief. It's evident
to everyone on hand: the strangled, staccato bursts,
the troubled breathing. Hang in there, old son, you've rehearsed
too long and hard to get tangled up in sentiment now.
There, there, you're beginning to calm down. We're all relieved,
even me, and I'm dead. Behold, Aggrievius, in full sail,
canvas snapping in the wind as we approach his peroration.
It's true, you know, I really was a decent chap, underneath:
kind to dogs, shop clerks – and something of a wit, to boot.
You trot out a few of my *bons mots* to make that very point, suggesting
that my more fierce or pungent asides are better left shelved
for now. – *Ho, ho, ho*, the assembled murmur, demurely.
A few of the best were at your expense, but we'll let that go.
You would have filed in, the lot of you, to Biber's *Rosary Sonatas*,
the Crucifixion part, 'Agony in the Garden,' all that.
Hardly the soundtrack, one would have guessed, for an old, dead Jew.
Quite a few of these chicks on hand have it going on still, eh?
You'd really have to blow it big time not to get laid,
what with all the tears, perfume, black lace… Am I being awful?
Forgive me. But it is my party, after all. *After all*, after all.
I'd say, on balance, it was a very nice show. In fact,
I might as well have scripted it myself, perhaps with better pacing.
But I could not have improved upon your speech, Aggrievius, no.
It really is you, finally, who knew me best and loathed me most.

Neetha Kunaratnam

The Afterlife

After every war
someone has to clean up. Things won't
straighten themselves up, after all
              Wisława Szymborska,
              'The End and the Beginning'

And someone will have to clean up,
but this is no job for ordinary Joes,
only specialists padded in moon boots,
face masks, and white chemical suits,

so someone will have to write a cheque
for the foreign input, the expertise
and expensive equipment:
the mine detectors and nerve sensors.

Somebody will need to order them
from the catalogue, ignore the new
solar-powered, GPS models, choose
the standard, remote-controlled breed,

as faithful and expendable as someone
sought to cordon off the area, skirt the perimeters
on tiptoe, mark out the dimensions
of the operation with sniffer dogs in tow.

Someone will need to believe the aggrieved
can make a difference, pray in numbers, petition
our leaders to subsidize farmers who can no
longer reap lest they're blown into thin air...

Someone will have to locate, then collect
any bright packages dropped after
the bombers droned off into the night,
their black boxes still replaying screams,

and someone sort out the dried food
from the prosthetic limbs, filter out the notes
of explanation, decipher a rationale
from the mistakes made in translation.

Someone will have to point out
that mustard leaves might not survive the blasts,
and checking they've turned red might set off
a barrage of blinding and a cluster of regrets.

Somebody will have to teach the children
that these M&M's aren't filled with peanuts
but pack an almighty punch. Explain that
a bomb as small as a battery can turn a sheep into a cloud.

James Lasdun

Stones

I'm trying to solve the problem of the paths
between the beds. A six-inch cover
of cedar chips that took a month to lay
rotted in two years and turned to weeds.
I scraped them up and carted them away,
then planted half a sack of clover seeds
for a 'living mulch'. I liked that: flowers
strewn along like stars, the cupid's bow
drawn on each leaf like thumbnail quartermoons,
its easy, springy give – until it spread
under the split trunks framing off each bed,
scribbling them over in its own
green graffiti… I ripped it out
and now I'm trying to set these paths in stone.
It isn't hard to find: the ground here's littered
with rough-cut slabs, some of them so vast
you'd think a race of giants must have lived here
building some bluestone Carnac or Stonehenge,
us their dwindled offspring, foraging
among their ruins… I scavenge
lesser pieces; pry them from the clutches
of tree-roots, lift them out of ditches,
filch them from our own stone wall
guiltily, though they're mine to take,
then wrestle them on board the two-wheeled dolly
and drag them up the driveway to the fence,
where, in a precarious waltz, I tip
and twist them backward, tilting all their weight
first on one corner, then the other
and dance them slowly through the garden gate.
The hard part's next, piecing them together;
a matter of blind luck and infinite pains:
one eye open for the god-given fit –

this stone's jagged key to that one's lock –
the other quietly gauging how to fudge it:
split the difference on angles, cram the gaps
with stone-dust filler; hoping what the rains
don't wash away, the frost will pack and harden…
A chipmunk blinks and watches from his rock,
wondering if I've lost my mind perhaps.
Perhaps I have; out here every day,
cultivating – no, not even that;
tending the inverse spaces of my garden
(it's like a blueprint now, for Bluebeard's castle),
while outside, by degrees, the planet slips
– a locking piece – into apocalypse,
but somehow I can't tear myself away:
I like the drudgery; I seem to revel
in pitting myself against the sheer
recalcitrance of the stones; using
their awkwardness – each cupped or bulging face,
every cockeyed bevel and crooked curve,
each quirk of outline (this one a cracked lyre,
that one more like a severed head) –
to send a flickering pulse along the border
so that it seems to ripple round each bed
with an unstonelike, liquid grace:
'the best stones in the best possible order'
or some such half-remembered rule in mind,
as if it mattered, making some old stones
say or be anything but stone, stone, stone;
as if these paths might serve some purpose
aside from making nothing happen; as if
their lapidary line might lead me somewhere –
inward, onward, upward, anywhere
other than merely back where I began,
wondering where I've been, and what I've done.

Hannah Lowe

Dance Class

The best girls posed like poodles at a show
and Betty Finch, in lemon gauze and wrinkles,
swept her wooden cane along the rows
to lock our knees in place and turn our ankles.
I was a scandal in that class, big-footed
giant in lycra, joker in my tap shoes,
slapping on the off-beat while a hundred
tappers hit the wood. I missed the cues
each time. After, in the foyer, dad,
a black man, stood among the Essex mothers
clad in leopard skin. He'd shake his keys
and scan the bloom of dancers where I hid
and whispered to another ballerina
he's the cab my mother sends for me.

Lorraine Mariner

Strangers

Those people who talk
to strangers
who make eye contact
with absolutely anyone –

their souls have a lid
perhaps or lashes
some form of protection
because most people

are not to be trusted
and how do they cope
with the brightness
when they are?

Glyn Maxwell

The Byelaws

Never have met me, know me well,
tell all the world there was little to tell,
say I was heavenly, say I was hell,
harry me over the blasted moors
        but come my way, go yours.

Never have touched me, take me apart,
trundle me through my town in a cart,
figure me out with the aid of a chart,
finally add to the feeble applause
        and come my way, go yours.

Never have read me, look at me now,
get why I'm doing it, don't get how,
other way round, have a rest, have a row,
have skirmishes with me, have wars,
        O come my way, go yours.

Never have left me, never come back,
mourn me in miniskirts, date me in black,
undress as I dress, when I unpack pack
yet pause for eternity on all fours
        to come my way, go yours.

Never have met me, never do,
never be mine, never even be you,
approach from a point it's impossible to
at a time you don't have, and by these byelaws
        come my way, go yours.

Kei Miller

Establishing the Metre

Like tailors who must know their clients' girths
   two men set out to find the sprawling measure of the earth.
     They walked the curve from Rodez to Barcelona,
       and Barcelona to Dunkirk. Such a pilgrimage!
        They did not call it inches, miles or chains –
         this distance which as yet had no clear name.
          Between France and Spain they dared to stretch
          uncalibrated measuring tapes. And foot
         by weary foot, they found a rhythm
          the measure that exists in everything.

JO Morgan

When he wakes...

When he wakes each day he winds his watch.
The notched crown growing stubborn as
the hair-thin spring inside is coiled tight.

A precision piece, special issue for navigators,
chronographic. Its circular motions divided,
subdivided, portioned out on separate dials.

At the back of the briefing room he winds it.
The webbing unbuckled, slipped from his slender wrist.
The bright steel poised between his fingertips.

A five-loop strap in airforce grey, the scratchy nylon
softened up by sweat, by daily grime.
He cleans the casing with a cotton bud.

When there is radio-silence he winds it.
The backward ratchet tick held up to his ear outdoing
the thrum of propellers, the hurricane hiss of the air.

Its sweep-hand zeroed with a double click.
Its distance-measure matched to universal machinations
echoed by its dark insides.

When settling down for bed he winds it,
glimpsing the sharp green glow of its dials
in putting out the light.

Each minute mark, each stuttering hand,
adorned with dabs of luminescent paint.
The stored-up brightnesses of day now softly given back.

David Morley

FURY

I love talking.
Tyson Fury, British Romany professional boxer

The fight's over. My corner-man and cut-man
are mist and water, mist and slaughter.
I scream at the crowd and swagger to the exit.
I bow my face in a locker-room mirror,
and to the mirror behind my eyes.
Infinity. A million beaten faces
stare out, blazing back at me,
brains black-puddinged from pummelling.
My fists are beating the locker door.
I am fighting-royalty. I have Gypsy
kings on both sides of the family.
My three brothers are the same as me.
With us, everyone is a tough guy.
They don't talk like you and me
are talking. But we all cry instantly.
Look at me: 6 feet 9. If someone
said this to me in my family,
I would just cry. All of us would.
But nothing's talked about in our family.
We just push each other aside,
or give each other a punch.
We don't bow to any man.
The red mist rises, an invisible
cloak around my ringside robe.
We won't bow to you.
I bow to the red mist, naked as fury.
It's not about the money fights.
It's the love of one-on-one combat,
the ring entrances, the talking.
I'm the Master of It all.

When I go in there, I'm trying
to put my fist through the back
of his head. To break his ribs,
make them sob out the other side.
Final bell. I bow to the mist, being gone.
I feel a chill burning my skin.
When the red mist rises, I see
their faces, as many as my mind's eye
can remember. I'd give my right arm
for any man who stays on his toes.
I'm in control when out of control.
The best style is no style.
You take a little something from everything,
use what works, chuck the rest out the ring.
My game's to get your man on the ground –
sprawl-and-brawl, grind-and-pound.
Gum-shield and teeth, they're one to me.
Once down, don't get up from your knees.
This is not your celeb boxing.
It's felling the other chancer in the ring
short of butchering the bastard
before he gets his breath back,
before he begs for no more.
One clean blow and the mist
will part for him. My opponent begs
for mercy. What's that, pal?
I'm Fury. Who's this Mercy?
The breath goes up from the beaten
ghost of a man. Submission.
I'll tell you who Fury is.
Eye to eyeball at the mirror;
breath on the screen while I scream
at replays on my iPad.
Pal,
one minute I'm inside the sun
and the next I'm in my car, gunning it
into a wall at a hundred miles an hour.

I don't trust you as far as I could
throw you. I don't trust myself.
I bought a brand-new Ferrari
in the summer of 2016.
I was bombing up the motorway
got the beast up to 190mph
heading smack towards a bridge.
I heard a voice crying,
your kids, your family,
your sons and daughter
growing up without their dad.
Before I turned into the bridge
I skidded back on the hard shoulder.
I have been so dark everything was pitch-black.
The fight's over. My corner-man and cut-man
are mist and water, mist and slaughter.
There is a name for what I am. I scream it
at the crowd and stagger to the exit.

Sinéad Morrissey

The Coal Jetty

Twice a day,
   whether I'm lucky enough
      to catch it or not,

the sea slides out
   as far as it can go
      and the shore coughs up

its crockery: rocks,
   mussel banks, beach glass,
      the horizontal chimney stacks

of sewer pipes,
   crab shells, bike spokes.
      As though a floating house

fell out of the clouds
   as it passed
      the city limits,

Belfast bricks, the kind
   that also built the factories
      and the gasworks,

litter the beach.
   Most of the landing jetty
      for coal's been washed

away by storms; what stands –
   a section of platform
      with sky on either side –

is home now to guillemots
   and cormorants
      who call up

the ghosts of nineteenth-
   century hauliers
      with their blackened

beaks and wings.
   At the lowest ebb,
      even the scum at the rim

of the waves
   can't reach it.
      We've been down here

before, after dinner,
   picking our way
      over mudflats and jellyfish

to the five spiked
   hallways underneath,
      spanned like a viaduct.

There's the stink
   of rust and salt,
      of cooped-up

water just released
   to its wider element.
      What's left is dark and quiet –

barnacles, bladderwrack,
   brick – but book-ended
      by light,

as when Dorothy
   opens her dull
      cabin door

and what happens outside is Technicolor.

Paul Muldoon

Pelt

Now rain rattled
the roof of my car
like holy water
on a coffin lid,
holy water and mud
landing with a thud

though as I listened
the uproar
faded to the stoniest
of silences… They piled
it on all day
till I gave way

to a contentment
I'd not felt in years,
not since that winter
I'd worn the world
against my skin,
worn it fur side in.

Les Murray

High-speed Bird

At full tilt, air gleamed –
and a window-struck kingfisher,
snatched up, lay on my palm
still beating faintly.

Slowly, a tincture
of whatever consciousness is
infused its tremor, and
ram beak wide as scissors

all hurt loganberry inside,
it crept over my knuckle
and took my outstretched finger
in its wire foot-rings.

Cobalt wings, shutting on beige
body. Gold under-eye whiskers,
beak closing in recovery
it faced outward from me.

For maybe twenty minutes
we sat together, one on one,
as if staring back or
forward into prehistory.

Daljit Nagra

A Black History of the English-Speaking Peoples

I

A king's invocations at the Globe Theatre
spin me from my stand to a time when boyish
       bravado and cannonade
and plunder were enough to woo the regal seat.

That the stuff of Elizabethan art and a nation
of walled gardens in a local one-up manship
       would tame the four-cornered
world for Empire's dominion seems inconceivable.

Between the birth and the fire and rebirth of the Globe
the visions of Albion led to a Rule Britannia
       of trade-winds-and-Gulf-Stream
all-conquering fleets that aroused theatres

for lectures on Hottentots and craniology,
whilst Eden was paraded in Kew.
       Between *Mayflower* and *Windrush*
(with each *necessary murder*) the celebrated

embeddings of imperial gusto where jungles
were surmounted so the light of learning be spread
       to help sobbing suttees
give up the ghost of a husband's flaming pyre.

II

So much for yesterday, but today's time-honoured
televised clashes repeat the flag of a book burning
       and May Day's Mohican
Churchill and all that shock and awe

that brings me back to Mr Wanamaker's Globe.
An American's thatched throwback to the king
        of the canon! I watch the actor
as king, from the cast of masterful Robeson.

The crowd, too, seem a hotchpotch from the pacts
and sects of our ebb and flow. My forbears played
        their part for the Empire's quid
pro quo by assisting the rule and divide of their ilk.

Did such relations bear me to this stage?
Especially with Macaulay in mind, who claimed the passing
        of the imperial sceptre would highlight
the imperishable empire of our arts...

So does the red of Macaulay's map run through
my blood? Am I a noble scruff who hopes a proud
        academy might canonise
his poems for their faith in canonical allusions?

Is my voice phoney over these oft-heard beats?
Well if my voice feels vexatious, what can I but pray
        that it reign Bolshie
through puppetry and hypocrisy full of gung-ho fury!

III

The heyday Globe incited brave new verse
modelled on the past, where time's frictions
        courted Shakespeare's corruptions
for tongue's mastery of the pageant subject. Perhaps

the Globe should be my muse! I'm happy digging
for my England's good garden to bear again.
        My garden's only a state
of mind, where it's easy aligning myself with a 'turncoat'

T. E. Lawrence and a *half-naked fakir* and always
the groundling. Perhaps to aid the succession
   of this language of the world,
for the poet weeding the roots, for the debate

in ourselves, now we're bound to the wheels
of global power, we should tend the manorial
   slime – that legacy
offending the outcasts who fringe our circles.

  IV

Who believes a bleached yarn? Would we openly
admit the Livingstone spirit turned Kurtz, our flag
   is a union of black and blue
flapping in the anthems of haunted rain…?

Coming clean would surely give us greater distance
than this king at the Globe, whose head seems cluttered
   with golden-age bumph,
whose suffering ends him agog at the stars.

  V

I applaud and stroll toward Westminster,
yet softly tonight the waters of Britannia bobble
   with flotillas of tea and white gold
cotton and sugar and the sweetness-and-light

blood lettings and ultimately red-faced Suez.
And how swiftly the tide removes from the scene
   the bagpipe clamouring
garrisons with the field-wide scarlet soldiery

and the martyr's cry: *Every man die at his post!*
Till what's ahead are the upbeat lovers who gaze
   from the London Eye
at multinationals lying along the sanitised Thames.

Sharon Olds

Departure Gate Aria

She was standing near a departure gate,
sandal-footed, her wiggly hair
and the latticework of her mercury footwear
the same satiny gold, and there was something
wistful about her, under the burnish
of her makeup she looked extremely young,
and a little afraid. I wanted to speak
to her, as if I were a guardian spirit
working the airport – God knows
I was crazed with my fresh solitariness –
so I did a little double take,
when I passed her, and said, Could I ask, where did you
get your sandals – my husband, I lied,
wants me to get some, and she said a name, as if
relieved to speak. Thanks, I said,
they look great with your hair – actually
(my head bowed down on its own), you look
like a goddess. Her face came out from behind
its cloud, You don't know how I needed that!,
she cried out, I'm going to meet my boyfriend's
parents. You'll do just fine, I said, you look
beautiful and good. She looked joyful. I bustled off –
so this is what I'll do, now,
instead of kissing and being kissed, I'll
go through airports praising people, like an
Antichrist saying, You do not need
to change your life.

Alice Oswald

Slowed-Down Blackbird

Three people in the snow
getting rid of themselves
        breath by breath

and every six seconds a blackbird

three people in raincoats losing their tracks in the snow
walking as far as the edge and back again
with the trees exhausted
        tapping at the sky

and every six seconds a blackbird

first three then two
passing one eye between them
and the eye is a white eraser rubbing them away

and on the edge a blackbird
trying over and over its broken line
trying over and over its broken line

Abigail Parry

The Quilt

The quilt's a ragtag syzygy
of everything I've been or done,
a knotted spell in every seam,
the stuff that pricks and pulls. The quilt

began in '96. I scrapped
the blotch batiks and brocatelles
each backward-bending paisley hook
that tied me to my town. The quilt

came with me when I packed and left
– a bad patch, that – you'll see I've sewn
a worried blot of grey and black
to mark a bruisy year. The quilt

advances, in a shock campaign
through block-fluorescent souvenirs
of seedy clubs and bad psytrance
and peters out in blue. The quilt

came with me when I ditched the scene
and dressed myself as someone new
– or someone else, at any rate
and someone better, too – I felt

a charlatan in borrowed suits,
and flower prints, and pastel hues,
but things had turned respectable,
and so I stitched that in. The quilt

has tessellated all of it.
Arranged, like faithful paladins,
are half a dozen bits and scraps
from those who took a turn, then split –

the dapper one, the rugby fan,
the one who liked his gabardine,
the one who didn't want to be   *another patch in your fucking quilt*
but got there all the same. The quilt

is lined with all the bitter stuff
I couldn't swallow at the time –
the lemon-yellow calico
I never wore again. The guilt

snuck into every thread of it
and chafed all through the honeymoon.
I scissored out the heart of it
and stitched it, fixed it, final, here –

with every other bright mistake
I wear, like anyone.

Don Paterson

Mercies

She might have had months left of her dog-years,
but to be who? She'd grown light as a nest
and spent the whole day under her long ears
listening to the bad radio in her breast.
On the steel bench, knowing what was taking shape
she tried and tried to stand, as if to sign
that she was still of use, and should escape
our selection. So I turned her face to mine,
and seeing only love there – which, for all
the wolf in her, she knew as well as we did –
she lay back down and let the needle enter.
And love was surely what her eyes conceded
as her stare grew hard, and one bright aerial
quit making its report back to the centre.

Pascale Petit

Green Bee-eater

More precious than all
the gems of Jaipur –

the green bee-eater.

If you see one singing
tree-tree-tree

with his space-black bill
and rufous cap,

his robes
all shades of emerald

like treetops glimpsed
from a plane,

his blue cheeks,
black eye-mask

and the delicate tail streamer
like a plume of smoke –

you might dream
of the forests

that once clothed
our flying planet.

And perhaps his singing
is a spell

to call our forests back –

tree
    by *tree*
        by *tree*.

Phoebe Power

notes on climate change

READING

The more I read on the subject, the more I find I need to know about economics, politics, geography and science. But these are areas I barely studied at school. I am trained to respond to texts: literature, music, the visual arts. Thankfully, I am equipped with the skills to scan and comprehend the main points of articles; this allows me better to understand, but not to do.

BLACKOUT

Coal/oil/gas needs to stay put, in the ground. Reduce emissions to zero.

What if a magician clapped his white-gloved hands and all the machines stopped their cranking and burring, mechanical arms stilled? Stage goes black. Combustion stops.

—

Then chaos; conflict; money wars; people with backyard generators running out to chop wood for fires

—

We could accept the proposition of some of the major religions that the self is nothing. We could let go of the self and allow it to dissolve. With this in mind, changes that are coming are nothing more than a great wave. We wait, death grows towards us and widens its embrace. We don't panic but are still, and it carries us away, at some time or another.

—

But the religions also teach us to save others, before thinking of our own death. Because the world is full of creatures who did not play a part in this.

—

I skip the paragraph on extinction. Yes, so this will happen… 40% of species wiped out (mosquitoes remain, spreading malaria. I hardly ever see them anyway). Birds, a fox sometimes. In the country, sheep. If I want to look at reefs or pangolins I can always stream them.

—

If you're a victim of childhood obesity or an eating disorder, then you will have other things to think about.

—

Fred is thinking about how to make his day in the office stuck to the computer bearable. He's already stopped for lunch and snacked on a couple of Jaffa Cakes. He's meeting Sara after work; he'll also have to find time to pick up supper from the supermarket; for example, a salmon en croûte. He's going to download the game he wants now online while he should be working. If he's got the motivation tomorrow he should get to the gym before work. That'll make him feel good and closer to perfect; at least, closer to OK.

—

Even if your house has been flooded you have other things to consider, such as whether you should move, and also, what kind of new kitchen units you and your husband both like.

—

John thinks, when he gets back to England from travelling he'll buy a little second-hand car to run around in. Who are you to say he shouldn't have it?

In general, times when we are able to find happiness correlate with omission of the subject. Most activities function perfectly well without its consideration. Outside work, we can even buy lunch out or a cake and coffee, go out for drinks, purchase a book or record. We can relax in a spa or book a plane ticket to a lesser-known European city, thereby providing a pleasant interruption to the routine and something new to photograph.

—

We can even grow fruit, keep chickens and bees, cook together and have sex. We can wander on mountains, draw or paint the colours and shapes we see around us, sing or join a band. We can learn languages, read about other cultures, or take on Proust. We can learn a skill, like knitting, papermaking or cake decoration. We can go camping, do a cycle trail. We can use the internet to share opinions and keep up to date. We can do this without remembering the subject. We can do most of these things without really thinking.

—

Actually, it crops up. In this part of Austria it crops up whitely, in the absence of snow. A 17-year-old boy told me of his ambition to be a ski instructor. He spends his holidays teaching on the slopes and is paid €200 a day. He loves skiing. But there are fewer and fewer instructors here. This winter was wetter, Christmas was wrong. At the February carnival, one float was painted with unsaid words like the silent victim of a strangling – *Wann wird es wieder richtiges Winter?*

—

In this small town, the elderly walk about over-hot in their antique furs and wool caps pinned with birds' feathers. Maybe a few days a winter, now, can Frau Stellinger put on her best sleek fur to go around town. She takes it off once she's reached the warm bank for her appointment.

On the dry road surface, some triangles of green
bottle glass flash yellow-white with bending rays.
Till rocks melt wi' the sun, my dear,
Till rocks melt.

Shivanee Ramlochan

On the Third Anniversary of the Rape

Don't say Tunapuna Police Station.
Say you found yourself in the cave of a minotaur, not
knowing how you got there, with a lap of red thread.
Don't say forced anal entry.
Say you learned that some flowers bloom and die
at night. Say you remember stamen, filament,
cross-pollination, say that hummingbirds are

vital to the process.

Give the minotaur time to write in the police ledger. Lap
the red thread
around the hummingbird vase.

Don't say I took out the garbage alone and he grabbed me by the
    waist and he was handsome.
            Say Shakespeare. Recite Macbeth for the tropics.
Lady Macbeth was the Queen of Carnival
and she stabbed Banquo with a vagrant's shiv during J'ouvert.
She danced a blood dingolay and gave her husband
    a Dimanche Gras upbraiding.

I am in mud and glitter so far steeped
    that going back is not an option.
Don't say rapist.

Say engineer of aerosol deodorant because pepper spray is illegal,
anything is illegal
Fight back too hard, and it's illegal,
>your nails are illegal

Don't say you have a vagina, say
he stole your insurance policy/ your bank boxes/ your first car
downpayment

Say
he took something he'll be punished for taking,
not something you're punished for holding
like red thread between your thighs.

Claudia Rankine

The New Therapist Specializes...

The new therapist specializes in trauma counseling. You have only ever spoken on the phone. Her house has a side gate that leads to a back entrance she uses for patients. You walk down a path bordered on both sides with deer grass and rosemary to the gate, which turns out to be locked.

At the front door the bell is a small round disc that you press firmly. When the door finally opens, the woman standing there yells, at the top of her lungs, Get away from my house! What are you doing in my yard?

It's as if a wounded Doberman pinscher or a German shepherd has gained the power of speech. And though you back up a few steps, you manage to tell her you have an appointment. You have an appointment? she spits back. Then she pauses. Everything pauses. Oh, she says, followed by, oh, yes, that's right. I am sorry.

I am so sorry, so, so sorry.

Vidyan Ravinthiran

A Chair Addresses Jackie Chan

As you somersault into my seat and spin
my legs in a henchman's face, I know
I love you, always have… Though one
might consider ours an abusive relationship.
Your own bruises, do they remember
how I held you, moved just as you desired
– or am I simply more of the scenery
bullets chewed to make that crucial
inch between my splintering flesh
and yours enthralling as the Gaza Strip
played for laughs? You are the realist
and I am a piece of your code, the mundane
detail which makes this room appear
an actual room in which to live and fight
to keep well-wrought urns from tottering
off their improbably thin pedestals,
holding before your face the explosive vest
so the gun-toting tough is comically arrested.
Yet I know my worth. I know you
have nightmares, of empty rooms, with no
urns or kitchen sinks or silly little chairs
to work with. There, your kung-fu bricolage
shrivels to nothing like the limbs of a saint.

Denise Riley

After La Rochefoucauld

'It is more shameful to distrust your friends
Than be deceived by them': things in themselves
Do hold – a pot, a jug, a jar, Sweet Williams'
Greenshank shins – so that your eye's pulled
Clear of metallic thought by the light constancy
Of things, that rest there with you. Or without.
That gaily deadpan candour draws you on –
Your will to hope rises across their muteness.

Michael Symmons Roberts

Footfall

In the minutes after birth, when midwives
do their weighing, swaddling, when they
hand you to your mother for your first suck,
all your shoes line up outside the room:

tiny soft-cloth purses, straight-laced
school brogues, one-night pairs you hired
for bowling, ice-skates, thigh boots, killer heels,
right through to soft again – misshapen slippers.

There is mercy in this moment,
so fleeting that your mother, father, never walk
the line, nor see it falter into sole-holed poverty,
or stop halfway with an immaculate stiletto.

Besides, you cannot read the runes from shoes.
You might become an actor, a dictator, barefoot
centenarian, a rumour, a ghost, a name in a book.

Roger Robinson

Trinidad Gothic

Some of the women in Point Ligoure had already been arrested
for seasoning their husbands' food with a pinch of cement powder.
A stone grew. Grit in an oyster. Chalk in a rooster's gizzard.
Within two weeks they lay dead with a wolf's stone in their stomachs.

The women all had a good reason for this mode of murder
and passed the method on to other women with the same cause.
But alas, too many men of Point Ligoure died at once,
which prompted an investigation, which led to a mass autopsy,

and flaps of stomachs peeled back to find stone after stone,
which led to aunties, grandmothers and girlfriends being led
away in daydresses and handcuffs as other women looked on.
But one clever woman in Point Ligoure found a new way.

You leave an iron out overnight, then before sunrise
you pummel the base of that iron into the soles
of his feet, and you cause an instant untraceable heart attack.
At Point Ligoure, you'll see a dozen irons glinting in the moonlight.

Stephen Santus

In a Restaurant

This gesture I make to ask for the bill,
Writing on the air
With an imaginary ballpoint,
I learnt from Christopher,
Who learnt it from his father,
Who learnt it himself somewhere.

Christopher's father is long dead:
He echoes less and less.
How strange that what survives of us
Is what we would hardly guess.

Stephen Sexton

Front Door

In through the translucent panels of the front door stained with
    roses
here and there their green stems wander sun patterns the
    cavernous hall
with rose outlines the wood paneled box came sharp-cornered
    the TV
so heavy to look at it cut into my clavicle was it
full of cannonballs and was it carried on four or six or eight
sets of shoulders into the room such impossible heaviness
for the size of it and was it full of tinctures puzzled colours
picture elements their sweep rates flashing across it when I saw
my reflection in the blackness of its face it was a child's face.
Neighbours came over their fences a summer day but dark with
    storms:
a deluge impassible roads the forest lurching on the hill.
I felt my head turn into stone no it wasn't the old TV
we carried her to the window the meteors that time of year
Perseids only sparks really the Irish Sea fell from the sky
in bullets through the afternoon and Kong Kappa no King Koopa
navigates his ship through the storm an engine or thunder rumbles.
Electrons pooled under the clouds the room was heavy with ions.
I held my breath in the lightning the sea fell into the garden.
Evening rose like the river then the flash with all of us in it
and her voice moves around the edge of the world and now I
    think I
remember what I mean to say which is only to say that once
when all the world and love was young I saw it beautiful glowing
once in the corner of the room once I was sitting in its light.

Jo Shapcott

Bees

I Tell the Bees

He left for good in the early hours with just
one book, held tight in his left hand:
The Cyclopedia of Everything Pertaining
to the Care Of the Honey-Bee; Bees, Hives,
Honey, Implements, Honey-Plants, Etc.
And I begrudged him every single et cetera,
every honey-strainer and cucumber blossom,
every bee-wing and flown year and dead eye.
I went outside when the sun rose, whistling
to call out them as I walked towards the hive.
I pressed my cheek against the wood, opened
my synapses to bee hum, I could smell bee hum.
'It's over, honies,' I whispered, 'and now you're mine.'

The Threshold

I waited all day for tears and wanted them, but
there weren't tears. I touched my lashes and
the eyewater was not water but wing and fur
and I was weeping bees. Bees on my face,
in my hair. Bees walking in and out of my
ears. Workers landed on my tongue
and danced their bee dance as their sisters
crowded round for the knowledge. I learned
the language too, those zig-zags, runs and circles,
the whole damned waggle dance catalogue.
So nuanced it is, the geography of nectar,
the astronomy of pollen. Believe me,
through my mouth dusted yellow
with their pollen, I spoke bees, I breathed bees.

The Hive

The colony grew in my body all that summer.
The gaps between my bones filled
with honeycomb and my chest
vibrated and hummed. I knew
the brood was healthy, because
the pheromones sang through the hive
and the queen laid a good
two thousand eggs a day.
I smelled of bee bread and royal jelly,
my nails shone with propolis.
I spent my days freeing bees from my hair,
and planting clover and bee sage and
woundwort and teasel and borage.
I was a queendom unto myself.

Going About With the Bees

I walked to the city carrying the hive inside me.
The bees resonated my ribs: by now
my mouth was wax, my mouth was honey.
Passers-by with briefcases and laptops
stared as bees flew out of my eyes and ears.
As I stepped into the bank the hum
increased in my chest and I could tell the bees
meant business. The workers flew out
into the cool hall, rested on marble counters,
waved their antennae over paper and leather.
'Lord direct us.' I murmured, then felt
the queen turn somewhere near my heart,
and we all watched, two eyes and five eyes,
we all watched the money dissolve like wax.

CCD

My body broke when the bees left,
became a thing of bones
and spaces and stretched skin.
I'd barely noticed
the time of wing twitch
and pheromone mismatch
and brood sealed in with wax.
The honeycomb they
left behind dissolved
into blood and water.
Now I smell of sweat and breath
and I think my body cells
may have turned hexagonal,
though the bees are long gone.

The Sting

When the wild queen leads the swarm
into the room, don't shut the door on them,
don't leave them crawling the walls, furniture
and books, a decor of moving fuzz. Don't go off
to the city, alone, to work, to travel underground.
The sting is no more *apis mellifera*, is a life
without honey bees, without an earful of buzz
an eyeful of yellow. The sting is no twin
waving antennae breaking through
the cap of a hatching bee's cell. The sting
is no more feral hive humming in the stone
wall of the house, no smell of honey
as you brush by. No bees will follow, not one,
and there lies the sting. The sting is no sting.

Danez Smith

dinosaurs in the hood

let's make a movie called *Dinosaurs in the Hood*.
Jurassic Park meets *Friday* meets *The Pursuit of Happyness*.
there should be a scene where a little black boy is playing
with a toy dinosaur on the bus, then looks out the window
& sees the *T. rex*, because there has to be a *T. rex*.

don't let Tarantino direct this. in his version, the boy plays
with a gun, the metaphor: black boys toy with their own lives
the foreshadow to his end, the spitting image of his father.
nah, the kid has a plastic brontosaurus or triceratops
& this is his proof of magic or God or Santa. i want a scene

where a cop car gets pooped on by a pterodactyl, a scene
where the corner store turns into a battleground. don't let
the Wayans brothers in this movie. i don't want any racist shit
about Asian people or overused Latino stereotypes.
this movie is about a neighborhood of royal folks—

children of slaves & immigrants & addicts & exile—saving their
    town
from real ass dinosaurs. i don't want some cheesy, yet progressive
Hmong sexy hot dude hero with a funny, yet strong, commanding
Black girl buddy-cop film. this is not a vehicle for Will Smith
& Sofia Vergara. i want grandmas on the front porch taking out
    raptors

with guns they hid in walls & under mattresses. i want those little
    spitty
screamy dinosaurs. i want Cecily Tyson to make a speech, maybe
    two.
i want Viola Davis to save the city in the last scene with a black
    fist afro pick
through the last dinosaur's long, cold-blood neck. But this can't be
a black movie. this can't be a black movie. this movie can't be
    dismissed

because of its cast or its audience. this movie can't be metaphor
for black people & extinction. This movie can't be about race.
this movie can't be about black pain or cause black pain.
this movie can't be about a long history of having a long history
    with hurt.
this movie can't be about race. nobody can say nigga in this movie

who can't say it to my face in public. no chicken jokes in this movie.
no bullet holes in the heroes. & no one kills the black boy. & no
    one kills
the black boy. & no one kills the black boy. besides, the only reason
i want to make this is for the first scene anyway: little black boy
on the bus with his toy dinosaur, his eyes wide & endless

                    his dreams possible, pulsing, & right there.

Tracy K Smith

Annunciation

I feel ashamed, finally,

Of our magnificent paved roads,

Our bridges slung with steel,

Our vivid glass, our tantalizing lights,

Everything enhanced, rehearsed,

A trick. I've turned old. I ache most

To be confronted by the real,

By the cold, the pitiless, the bleak.

By the red fox crossing a field

After snow, by the broad shadow

Scraping past overhead.

My young son, eyes set

At an indeterminate distance,

Ears locked, tuned inward, caught

In some music only he has ever heard.

Not our cars, our electronic haze.

Not the piddling bleats and pings

That cause some hearts to race.

Ashamed. Like a pebble, hard

And small, hoping only to be ground to dust

By something large and strange and cruel.

Jean Sprackland

Shepherdess and Swain

Cremated bones go into china,
and it is too brittle you would think for these
come-hither folds of cloth with all their warm suggestions.

He has one knee on the blue-and-white ground
and the other pressed to her skirt.
He raises one badly painted eyebrow.
She urges him on from the corner of a smudged mouth.
His hand is on his racing heart.
She is reaching to touch his arm.
And the dew rises through them.

No, it is the wrong stuff: all gloss
and deadpan, suitable for vases and teapots.
There is dust in all its clefts and curlicues,
and tapped with a fingernail it makes a cold note.

This belongs on a mantelpiece in a dismal sitting room
where the chimney will not draw; where someone
bored with a lifetime of unheard melodies
would come in and pick it up

and look at the boy cross-eyed with lust
and the poor girl flushed and impatient,
the two of them trapped in this rictus of desire

and no release, no way to pitch the story on
except to knock them onto the hearth and smash them.

Martha Sprackland

Pimientos de Padrón

Os pementos de Padrón
uns pican e outros non

A plateful of dark green bullets
slick in their lake of grassy blood
and charred from the fire,

still hissing and settling, smoking,
the skin lifting and curling
studded with salt-flakes.

They were our cheap roulette – *some hot,*
others not (the capsicum is brewed
by the sudden sun at summer's edge).

We were all of us bad at decisions,
lovesick, shamed or fleeing
or brisant and in shock. The city emptied

as the madrileños boarded up
the bodegas and rippled out
towards the cooler coasts

leaving us to our own boiling ghosts,
reckless enough to hold
the dare to our mouths, fire

or sweetness spreading across the tongue
and then head to the airport
for the first flight anywhere but home.

Julian Stannard

Trolley Man

When someone asks, Could I have
a sandwich with some cheese in it?
I will say No sandwiches today!

And if anyone should ask for coffee
I will say, Hot water not working.
Shocking, isn't it?

I will wheel my trolley from one end
of the train to the other, smiling
magnificently at everyone.

And when a lady asks,
I don't suppose you've got
a piece of shortbread
some lovely, lovely shortbread?

I will say, No my dear
all the lovely shortbread has gone.

Arundhathi Subramaniam

My Friends

They're sodden, the lot of them,
leafy, with more than a whiff
of damage,
mottled with history,
dark with grime.

God knows I've wanted them different –
less preoccupied, more jaunty,
less handle-with-care,

more airbrushed,
less prone
to impossible dreams, less perishable,

a little more willing
to soak in the sun.

They don't measure up.
They're unpunctual.
They turn suddenly tuberous.

But they matter
for their crooked smiles,
their endless distractions,
their sudden pauses –

signs that they know
how green stems twist

and thicken
as they vanish
into the dark,

making their way
through their own sticky vernacular tissues
of mud,

improvising,
blundering,
improvising –

George Szirtes

Actually, Yes

Somewhere between the highly spectacular *No*
and the modest *yes* of the creatures, word
arises and claims its space. *No* can afford
fireworks and a grand entrance, but *yes* must go
barefoot across floorboards. *No* can extend
its franchise over the glossolalia
of the imagination: *yes* discovers failure
in a preposition impossible to offend.
No demands success and receives reviews
of the utmost luminosity while *yes*
is damned with faint praise. *No* profits by excess:
yes has little to say and even less to lose.
The full Shakespearean ending is *No* with its raised brow.
Yes disappears off stage and will not take a bow.

Look, here's a very small *yes*. Now watch it run
its almost invisible race through nature. How
does it know where to go? Where is it now?
Right there! Just there! Like a picture of no one
in particular it looks surprised to be seeing
itself approach a selfhood hardly likely. See
it hesitate as it approaches the sheer possibility
of emergence on the very edge of being.
Always off-centre, its marginal affirmation
of life's distant provinces will be rewarded
with the briefest of smiles when smiles can be afforded
while monstrous *No* boldly addresses the nation.
But now and then, the honest citizen will confess,
when asked, to a weakness of sorts, whispering *Yes*.

Well, *yes*. Actually, *yes*.

Maria Taylor

Loop

Maybe time moves like a figure of eight,
surging forwards then back on itself.

Light returns from exploded stars.
A grown woman could turn a corner
and see herself crying as a girl.

Newsflash: our world ends again.
The disappearing forests of childhood
disappear again.
                            The path curves.

It takes the woman back to a dimly-lit bar
where she meets the same lover again and again.
She risks everything once more.

They've already met
before they've said a word.

Kae Tempest

Thirteen

The boys have football and skate ramps.
They can ride BMX
and play basketball in the courts by the flats until midnight.
The girls have shame.

One day,
when we are grown and we have minds of our own,
we will be kind women, with nice smiles and families and jobs.
And we will sit,
with the weight of our lives and our pain
pushing our bodies down into the bus seats,
and we will see thirteen-year-old girls for what will seem like the first
    time since we've been them,
and they will be sitting in front of us, laughing
into their hands at our shoes or our jackets,
    and rolling their eyes at each other.

While out of the window, in the sunshine,
the boys will be cheering each other on,
and daring each other to jump higher and higher.

Lucy Anne Watt

The Tree Position

My son went to war in a country the colour of sand. And came back
in a light beech box hefted on the shoulders of six strong men.

And this and my son turned me into a tree.
All the leaves of my happiness fell from me.

I hooked my fingers into the sky and my roots embraced
the last of my son. Earth to earth as they say.

But ash is the taste in my mouth. Ash, the colour of my sky and skin;
of the remains of my love. In parturition I did not scream.

I bit down hard on a towel, a rag, so as better to hear
my boy's first shout. As I embody his last that I never heard.

And I watched the Prime Minister pass. The young PM
aka Warlord, aka Sancho Panza to another's Quixote,

aka Pinball Player with the lives of young men. And I saw in him
        an actor.
An actor can act big while being a fool.

And even with my fingers in the sky, and my roots in cinders,
and rain always in my eyes, strung between

the hell of my love and the heaven of release,
suspended in the perpetual winter

of barrenness reprised,
the PM looked right through me. And I decided

Only lawyers think that wars are arguments to be won. But wars are
    always lost.
In the heart. In the home. In the wheelchair. In the widow's tiny
    portion.

In the fatherless child. In mothers
like me. In the compound nature of the cost.

Soldiers obey orders. But where were mine?
When did I contract to be as I now am?

So I cursed the PM. I will not say how. I was one
grieving tree. But the war goes on. I am a forest now.

Hugo Williams

From the Dialysis Ward

If I'm Early

Every other day I follow the route
of the Midland Railway
to where it cuts through
St Pancras Old Church Cemetery.
I might go into the church
and heave a sigh or two
before continuing via a gate
set in the cemetery wall
to the Mary Rankin Wing
of St Pancras Hospital.

As a young man, Thomas Hardy
supervised the removal of bodies
from part of the cemetery
to make way for the trains.
He placed the headstones
round an ash tree sapling,
now grown tall, where I stop sometimes
to look at the stones
crowding round the old tree
like children listening to a story.

A Game of Dialysis

The home team appears
in a blue strip, while the visitors
keep on their street clothes.
We find our positions
from the file with our name on it
placed beside our bed.
Now all we can do is wait
for the opposition to make a move.
We don't like our chances.

The action commences
with the home team wandering about,
or making a tour of the circuit.
Certain moves are typical –
lengthwise, for example,
carrying something,
is a popular move, or scoring points
by passing back and forth
between the glove dispenser
and the needle disposal box.

The visitors can only look on
as the enemy's game plan emerges.
We score by keeping quiet
about our disadvantages,
or saying something funny.
Whether anyone gets hurt
depends on who is marking whom.
The blues fan out round the room.
Each of them is doing something difficult
to somebody lying down.

The Art of Needling
You find out early on
that some of the nurses
are better than others
at the art of needling.
You have to ascertain

who's on duty
that knows what they're doing,
someone familiar
with your fistula arm
and beg him to 'put you on'.

If he's any good
he'll take his time

raising or lowering the bed,
laying out his things on the tray.
He won't forget the spray.

He'll listen to the 'bruit'
produced by your fistula.
He'll note the 'thrill' of it,
feel it with his finger.
Only then will he go in.

Even so, a wayward needle
can pierce a fistula wall,
causing a 'blow' to occur.
Then you have to go to A&E
for a fistulaplasty.

The Dog

A dog has got hold of my arm
and is dragging me down.
Its canines pierce an artery.
Its entrails twitch with my blood.

Whenever I am brought in
for further questioning,
the dog stands over me,
grinding its teeth in my flesh.

It's like being nailed to the floor
and told to relax.
Blood spurts like a confession.

This is what dogs are for,
to find out who you are.

I watch its eyes going round,
analysing the evidence.
I'll admit to anything.

The Angel of the Needles

The beauty of the Indian nurse
puts the fear of God in me
when she approaches my bed
carrying the blue tray.

Did she have to take a needling test
like other mortals?
Or did they let her in
for being one of the angels?

I want her to like me,
but I have to look away
when she strips the paper from the needles
and bends over me.

She applies the tourniquet
and lays a finger on the vein.
Something about her touch
makes the needles melt in my flesh.

She takes away the pain
by telling me in a mournful tone
about her son Ibrahim
who is bullied at school
for the mixed pigments on his face.

Ray's Way

Ray Blighter appears in the doorway
of the dialysis ward
in all his ruined finery –
waistcoat, buttonhole, blazer,
eyebrows dashed in with mascara –
and pauses for a moment to ensure
all eyes are upon him.

'MY NAME IS BOND' he shouts
to the assembled company.
'JAMES FUCKING BOND.'
He sets off down the line of beds,
muttering, looking straight ahead,
yellowing grey flannels
flapping round his ankles.

He's two hours late,
having been 'run over by a bus',
but God help anyone who's taken
his precious corner bed.
If the rabbi is there ahead of him
he's liable to turn around
and go home again.

He sets out his life
on the table across his bed –
beer cans, biscuits, betting slips,
a hairbrush, aftershave,
a radio tuned to Radio 2,
the only one allowed on the ward
because Ray is a 'character'.

He goes and stands in the fire exit
for his ritual 'last cigarette'
before he kills himself.
'Do you smoke Morland Specials
with the three gold rings?' I ask.
Ray lifts a coal-black eyebrow.
'Do you think I look like Sean Connery?'

He acted with Sean, he tells me,
in several James Bond films,
including *Live and Let Die*.
'And no, not as a bleeding extra!'

When he goes on to describe his role
in *Bridge on the Fucking River Kwai*
the penny drops.

Trapped in his own Japanese
prisoner-of-war camp for ten years,
he's lied and cursed his way free.
'I won't be coming in on Monday',
he tells me confidentially.
'I'm going to the fucking races.'
Of course he is. I may be there myself.

Diality

The shock of remembering,
having forgotten for a second,
that this isn't a cure,
but a kind of false health,
like drug addiction.

It performs the trick
of taking off the water
which builds up in your system,
bloating your body,
raising your blood pressure.

It sieves you clean of muck
for a day or two,
by means of a transparent tube
full of pinkish sand
hanging next to your machine.

Your kidneys like the idea
of not having to work any more
and gradually shut down,
leaving you dependent.
Then you stop peeing.

Dialysis is bad for you.
You feel sick
most of the time, until the end.
The shock of remembering,
having forgotten for a second.

Zombie

I'm technically dead, they tell me,
but I remember being alive
as if it were yesterday.
I'm covered in mud, like a zombie,
swimming around
in the storms of a new grave.

I remember the world above
and what it was like up there,
thanks to a friend
who sucks my blood for me.
He keeps me alive
in the sense that memories are alive.

Going Home

Leaving behind the Gothic frowns
of the former workhouse, I pass through a gate
into a churchyard overhung by great trees,
where the nurses go to smoke.

Mary Wollstonecraft's tomb,
where Shelley proposed to her daughter,
escaped demolition by Thomas Hardy
and seems to be plunging off into a storm.

Shelley's heart, wrapped in a brown paper parcel,
Hardy took by train to Bournemouth,
sitting in a first class compartment
with the heart on his knee.

Luke Wright

To London...

To London then, that fatted beast
on which the whole world comes to feast,
all private woe and public farce;
where money twerks its oiled arse
in gorgeous, fenced-off Georgian squares
and starchy oligarchical lairs;
where soaring, steel-glass towers sit
in ancient, ghoulish, plague-filled pits;
where gap-toothed roads left by the Blitz
are soaked in years of pigeon shit;
where listless folk roam airless malls
as slaves to airbrushed siren calls
then, gobsmacked, flash their plastic cash
and fill their hearts and lungs with ash;
where policy is signed and sealed
then forced upon the shires and fields;
where money men spin even more
from love of it and fear of war
(like bookie blokes they will their stocks
as food bank queues ring grotty blocks);
where cut-glass vowels meet glottal stops;
where half-cut kids in chicken shops
dream dreams as false as talent shows,
these rebels wrapped in branded clothes,
this lunar race illuminated
by their screens but never sated,
all within their reach at last
but safe behind the steel-laced glass –
it's oh so close but out of touch,
it's not for you, they know that much,
it's not for you, it's not for you,
it's not for you...
                    to London then.

Biographies

Patience Agbabi (b. 1965, London, UK) describes herself as a 'poetical activist'; her four collections rework time-honoured forms and revisit canonical authors to extract what's vital and timely from the tradition. Her updating of *The Canterbury Tales* – *Telling Tales* (Canongate, 2014) – came out of her work as Canterbury laureate; she's also been Poet in Residence for venues as diverse as Eton College, a tattoo parlour and the Brontë Parsonage Museum. In an interview with the Poetry Archive, she laid out her poetic credo: 'The written must be spoken. The chasm between page and stage must be healed.'

Mir Mahfuz Ali (b. 1958, Dhaka, Bangladesh) is a dancer, actor and performance artist, as well as a poet. His debut collection, *Midnight, Dhaka* (Seren, 2014), from which 'Hurricane' was taken, explores the Bangladesh of his youth with startling clarity in the face of trauma and suffering: he came to England after being shot by riot police in the throat. His first publication was in Bloodaxe's seminal anthology *Ten*, for which he was mentored by Pascale Petit. In 2013, he won the Geoffrey Dearmer Prize for his poem 'MIG-21 Raids at Shegontola'.

Raymond Antrobus (b. 1986, London, UK) has been writing poetry for as long as he can remember. 'I had permission to engage with it without the baggage that many people in the UK have, where poetry is solely associated with some negative experiences in English lessons at school,' he writes. 'I associate it with family and songs and solitude.' Antrobus was one of the first six graduates of Goldsmiths' MA in Spoken Word Education. His debut collection, *The Perseverance* (Penned in the Margins, 2019), explores themes including d/Deafness, fatherhood and marginalisation.

Simon Armitage (b. 1963, Marsden, UK) describes his first poetic experiences, staring from the bedroom window of the house he grew up in and had returned to after university, in the introduction to his latest book, *Magnetic Field: The Marsden Poems* (Faber & Faber, 2020): 'The village became the drawing board or board game on which I could practise my poetics and play out my perspectives.' Thirty years later, those perspectives have widened to the broad vistas of the UK laureateship and the Oxford Professorship of Poetry, but Armitage's work remains grounded in the local and near-at-hand.

Mona Arshi (b. 1970, London, UK) worked as a human rights lawyer for Liberty before she became a poet. She has described how both jobs require, at heart, 'a restless interrogation of language', an interrogation fully realised in her two collections from Pavilion Poetry, *Small Hands* (2015) and *Dear Big Gods* (2019). She is a deft formalist but rejects the idea that poetry requires specialist training to appreciate: 'Poetry,' she writes, 'is simply the world we live in, translated into language.'

Fatimah Asghar (b. 1990, Cambridge, MA, USA) is a Pakistani, Kashmiri, Muslim American writer. She is the co-creator of *Brown Girls*, an internet TV series celebrating friendships between women of colour, which was nominated for an Emmy. Her poetry, collected in *If They Come for Us* (Corsair, Little, Brown Book Group, 2019), won a prestigious Ruth Lilly and Dorothy Sargent Rosenberg Poetry Fellowship. 'Poems create a space for reinvention,' she has written, and reinvention and change are recurring themes in her work, whether internal or (as in 'Partition') colonial imposition.

Fiona Benson (b. 1978, Wroughton, UK) won the 2019 Forward Prize for Best Collection for *Vertigo & Ghost* (Cape Poetry), from which 'Eurofighter Typhoon' is taken. Charlotte Higgins, in a review for the *Guardian*, praised the way Benson brought to light 'the seam of dread that lurks just beneath the surface of our times'. But Benson is a tender poet, too: terror and tenderness are fitting poles for a poet who writes so sensitively and precisely about motherhood; they are also the key notes of her long sequences updating Ancient Greek mythology, a form she has made absolutely her own.

Tara Bergin (b. 1974, Dublin, Rep. of Ireland) is a lecturer in creative writing at Newcastle University. Her poems often have their genesis in notebook fragments: 'the definition of a word, a sentence spoken by a newsreader I liked the sound of, or sometimes a note about the atmosphere in someone else's poem.' Her PhD thesis is on the

Hungarian poet János Pilinszky and his influence on Ted Hughes, and her work often incorporates Eastern European motifs or models, as in 'Stag-Boy', which recreates and adapts Ferenc Juhász's poem 'The boy turned into a stag cries out at the gate of secrets'.

Emily Berry (b. 1981, London, UK) edits *The Poetry Review*. Her debut collection, *Dear Boy* (Faber & Faber, 2013), won the Forward Prize for Best First Collection; the 2017 follow-up, *Stranger, Baby* (from which 'Aura' is taken), explores in fractured and elliptical narratives what Berry has described as 'the long shadow cast by the loss of a mother in childhood – my own loss'.

Liz Berry (b. 1980, Black Country, UK), with the encouragement of her mentor Daljit Nagra, incorporated the Black Country dialect of her childhood into her poetry. The resulting collection, *Black Country* (Chatto, 2014) won the Forward Prize for Best First Collection. Berry's subsequent pamphlet, of which 'The Republic of Motherhood' is the title poem, explores the post-natal loneliness and tentative solidarities among new mothers.

Sujata Bhatt (b. 1956, Ahmedabad, Gujarat, India) emigrated with her family to America when she was 12; her first collection, *Brunizem* (Carcanet, 1988) won the Commonwealth Poetry Prize. Michael Schmidt has noted her 'complete imagination, generous and at the same time unsparingly severe in its quest for the difficult truths of experience'. In 1989 she moved to Bremen in North Germany, where she still lives.

Caroline Bird (b. 1986, Leeds, UK) published her first collection with Carcanet when she was just 15; since then, there have been five more, the most recent of which, *The Air Year*, won the 2020 Forward Prize for Best Collection. She is also a playwright, whose credits include *The Trial of Dennis the Menace* and a new translation of *The Trojan Women*. Bird has described her ideal poem as an 'amnesia injection which makes the world strange again': hers is a poetry of shifting perspectives, surrealistic images and unexpected destinations.

Malika Booker (b. 1970, London, UK) is co-founder with Roger Robinson of the writers' collective Malika's Poetry Kitchen. Her first collection, *Pepper Seed* (Peepal Tree, 2013), was shortlisted for the Seamus Heaney Centre Prize. She is a Creative Writing Teaching Fellow at the University of Leeds and was the first Poet in Residence at the Royal Shakespeare Company. Pascale Petit has praised her power of bearing witness, 'raw as chili peppers rubbed into a wound'.

Sean Borodale (b. 1973, London, UK) has described his practice as 'documentary poems'; his poetry is site-specific and grows out of screen-printed, performed and situated writings he calls 'lyrigraphs'. Each collection has a sharp individual focus: the insect life of *Inmates*; the interior of a Mendip quarry in *Asylum*; and the daily rhythms of beekeeping in *Bee Journal*, from which '10th February: Queen' was taken. Borodale trained at the Slade School of Fine Art and has made large-scale bronze sculptures for artists including Anish Kapoor, Tracey Emin and Gavin Turk.

Colette Bryce (b. 1970, Derry, Northern Ireland, UK) spent much of her twenties reading contemporary poetry while working as a bookseller in London. After publishing her first collection in 2000, Bryce won a literary fellowship and has worked as a writer and editor ever since. She is currently Creative Writing Fellow at University College, Dublin. Her poems make their home in contested terrain: mortality, loyalty and the national fault lines of a Northern Irish childhood are themes she returns to again and again.

John Burnside (b. 1955, Dunfermline, Scotland, UK) describes his Catholic childhood in Corby as solitary: 'Reading poetry was probably the only real education I had in anything.' He became a writer while working as a software engineer. His novels, memoirs and poems have won many awards, and his 2011 collection, *Black Cat Bone*, won both the Forward Prize for Best Collection and the TS Eliot Prize. Rachel Campbell-Johnson, writing in the *Times*, captures the unique quality of his attention: 'He doesn't just look: he watches. He sees into secret spaces that lie somewhere between the hidden and the revealed.'

Niall Campbell (b. 1984, South Uist, UK) grew up in the Outer Hebrides, whose seas and stillnesses formed the imaginative background for his debut collection, *Moontide* (Bloodaxe Books, 2014). The poems of its follow-up, *Noctuary*, were written in whatever moments he could snatch from the larger responsibilities of new parenthood; Suzannah V Evans, reviewing the collection for the *Times Literary Supplement*, described it as 'a passionately tender examination of what it means to have and care for a small child'.

Vahni Capildeo (b. 1973, Port of Spain, Trinidad and Tobago) has lived in the UK since 1991, studying Old Norse at Christ Church, Oxford, and working as an etymologist on the Oxford English Dictionary. Their third collection, *Measures of Expatriation* (Carcanet), won the Forward Prize for Best Collection in 2016. Many-tongued and multicultural, their work sweeps through long prose poems and short imagistic bursts, through surrealism and gritty realism, acutely seeking the right form for each individual thought.

Mary Jean Chan (b. 1990, Hong Kong) was shortlisted in 2017 for the Forward Prize for Best Single Poem, becoming the youngest shortlistee in the prize's history; she followed it up two years later with another shortlisting for 'The Window'. Her debut collection, *Flèche* (Faber & Faber), won the 2019 Costa Book Award for Poetry and was commended by the judges as 'a staggeringly beautiful mix of the personal and the political'.

Brendan Cleary (b. 1958, Carrickfergus, Northern Ireland, UK) moved from Northern Ireland to the northeast of England when he was 19, founding the Echo Room magazine and pamphlet press and taking over the influential Morden Tower poetry reading series. His work has been published in small press chapbooks and by larger publishers, including Bloodaxe Books and Pighog; it's distinguished by its evasion of anything self-consciously poetic, an insistence on the mundane and telling detail.

Loretta Collins Klobah (b. 1961, Merced, California, USA) received the OCM Bocas Prize in Caribbean Literature for her first collection, *The Twelve Foot Neon Woman* (Peepal Tree, 2011). She writes deeply rooted, sprawling poems, engaged in the communities, languages and traditions of the places she's lived: San Juan in Puerto Rico, the Caribbean islands, Peckham and Notting Hill in London. Carol Rumens, writing in the *Guardian*, has praised the rhythmic energy of her line – influenced by dance traditions, including bomba, plena, salsa, reggaetón and others – as well as the 'vividness of her scenes and the vernacular force of her diction'.

David Constantine (b. 1944, Salford, UK) is a novelist and short-story writer as well as a poet (his story '45 Years' was made into a film starring Charlotte Rampling and Tom Courtenay). For a long time, he edited the magazine *Modern Poetry in Translation*; his own translations, especially from the German, have fed into his original work, giving it an austereness and seriousness unusual in contemporary poetry. In 2020, Constantine was awarded the Queen's Gold Medal for Poetry.

Robert Crawford (b. 1959, Bellshill, Scotland, UK) is a poet of strong convictions: religious, as in the playful Biblical reworkings of *Testament* (Cape Poetry, 2014), and political, as in his poems for Scottish independence. Questions of language and voice are a recurrent fascination: he has translated Cavafy into Scots and the 17th-century Latin poet Arthur Johnston into English. With Mick Imlah in 2000, he edited the *Penguin Book of Scottish Verse*, to many the standard single-volume anthology of Scottish poetry. He is Professor of Poetry at the University of St Andrews.

Emily Critchley (b. 1980, Athens, Greece) is a senior lecturer at the University of Greenwich, specialising in experimental poetry. *Love / All That / & OK*, which gathered together her work from early small-press pamphlets along with new material, was published by Penned in the Margins in 2011. Critchley's poetry, praised by Allen Fisher for its 'high electrics', works to upend poetic conventions: lyric, confessional, pastoral. Her latest collection is a book of experimental poems and collages for children, *alphabet poem: for kids!* (Prototype, 2020), co-written with Michael Kindellan and Alison Honey Woods.

Nichola Deane (b. 1973, Bolton, UK) was selected by Carol Ann Duffy for her first round of 'Laureate's Choice' pamphlets. Explaining her choice, Duffy described Deane as a poet 'both sophisticated and lyrically charged who deploys imagery that is both precise and daring'. These qualities are well evidenced in her first full collection, *Cuckoo* (V Press, 2019). In an interview with the Poetry School, Deane emphasises how poetry evades commercialisation: 'a poem is never a product, even when it's in book form. A true poem always escapes the book to go to the heart, the mind, the thingness of things.'

Tishani Doshi (b. 1975, Chennai, India) is a dancer as well as a poet, and choreographed a dance routine from the title poem of her 2018 collection, *Girls Are Coming Out of the Woods*. 'It seemed to lend itself to using the body,' she says. The body, appropriately enough, has been one of her central preoccupations, from her Forward Prize-winning debut, *Countries of the Body*, onwards. She is also a novelist, journalist and biographer, and lives in a small village on the southeast coast of India.

Sarah Doyle (b. 1967, London, UK) is Poet in Residence at the Pre-Raphaelite Society. A PhD on the poetics of meteorology at Birmingham City University led to a first encounter with Dorothy Wordsworth's journals; a collection of poetry based on these journal entries, *Something so wild and new in this feeling*, was published by V Press in 2021. She has co-edited two themed poetry anthologies: *Dreaming Spheres: Poems of the Solar System* and *Humanagerie*, a collection of 'creaturely poems'.

Nick Drake (b. 1961, London, UK) has had a long career in theatre and cinema. He is a screenwriter and script editor and head of development at a large film company; he has worked on films including *Sliding Doors* and *The Quiet American*. In 2010, he travelled to the Arctic with the art organisation Cape Farewell to witness the effects of climate change; in the collections that followed, *The Farewell Glacier* and *Out of Range*, environmental concerns are foregrounded. Nancy Campbell, reviewing *Out of Range* for ClimateCultures, celebrated his poetry's 'poignancy, formal facility and immense honesty'.

Carol Ann Duffy (b. 1955, Glasgow, Scotland, UK) was the first female Poet Laureate of the United Kingdom in the post's 400-year history. 'Duffy is a popular poet, with the emphasis firmly on the poetry, not the popularity,' writes Liz Lochhead. The presence of 1993's *Mean Time* on the A-level English syllabus means Duffy is a formative influence on an entire generation of younger poets. She made her name as an adept re-invigorator of the dramatic monologue, but more recent collections have centered other forms of lyric, including *Rapture* (Picador Poetry, 2005), a collection of love poems to her then partner, the poet Jackie Kay.

Ian Duhig (b. 1954, London, UK) grew up among Irish expatriates in Kilburn and worked with homeless people for 15 years before becoming a full-time writer. Finding, as he writes, that 'location and poetry dissolve into each other for me', Duhig has inserted a rare depth of understanding of his native Leeds into his poetry. Formally, his particular talent is for the dramatic monologue – perhaps his most famous poem in this form, 'The Lammas Hireling', won the Forward Prize for Best Single Poem in 2001 – but he is also adept at more anonymous 'folk' forms, including ballads, work songs and shanties.

Kate Edwards (b. 1978, Black Country, UK) trained as an actor and clown in Paris, and subsequently set up an all-female theatre troupe, Jammy Voo, with her fellow graduates; the troupe has toured the UK and abroad and has an enthusiastic following in Algeria. She completed a MA in Creative Writing at Warwick University and works as a teacher in the Calder Valley.

Rhian Edwards (b. Bridgend, Wales, UK) won the Wales Book of the Year Award for her debut collection, *Clueless Dogs* (Seren, 2012). She started writing poetry after attending a reading at the Poetry Café in Covent Garden and has since become an in-demand performer of her own work, winning the John Tripp Award for Spoken Poetry in 2010. Joe Dunthorne has praised the subversive feminist narratives of her most recent collection, *The Estate Agent's Daughter*: 'Reading them feels like being led through beautiful rooms by an estate agent who always takes care to show you what's hidden beneath the floorboards.'

Helen Farish (b. 1962, Cumbria, UK) taught English as a foreign language in half a dozen cities: Ankara, Istanbul, Turin, Casablanca, Palermo and Thessaloniki. This experience of different vistas is immediately present in all three of her collections. *Nocturnes at Nohant* (Bloodaxe Books, 2012), for instance, reconstructs the relationship between Chopin and George Sand and is deeply embedded in the French countryside. Her first book was called *Intimates*, a title that brings together many of the threads in her work: intimacies with place, with the body, with memory.

Paul Farley (b. 1965, Liverpool, UK) takes the past as his central theme: memory and its distortions, his working-class childhood in Liverpool, the shifty transitional landscapes he explores in his non-fiction book *Edgelands* (with Michael Symmons Roberts). He has published five collections with Picador. Poetry, for him, is naturally an evasive form, resistant to being pinned down: 'As soon as you establish a rule, somebody will come along and break it effectively. As soon as you attempt a definition, you feel it starting to crumble in your mouth.'

Parwana Fayyaz (b. 1990, Kabul, Afghanistan) is a research fellow in Persian Studies at Peterhouse, Cambridge, focusing on the medieval poet Jami and the confluences between Eastern and Western literature. Her poem 'Forty Names', which won the Forward Prize for Best Single Poem in 2019, draws inspiration from those same medieval traditions: 'It is about a mountain called *kohi chehal dokhtaran*, the forty girls' mountain. My poem tries to re-narrate the story by giving the forty women their names, a lamp and their colourful scarves.'

Vicki Feaver (b.1943, Nottingham, UK) didn't begin writing seriously until her children went to school. 'A man at a party asked me, "What do you do in the afternoons?"', she writes. 'Desperate not to admit that I was a housewife, mother and typist for my then husband, I lied, "I'm a poet".' Her poetry over four collections, most recently *I Want! I Want!* (Cape Poetry, 2019), explores themes of female ambition, desire and its repression, in a lyric style described by Ted Hughes as 'thin, beautifully etched ice – over such deep shocking water'.

Leontia Flynn (b. 1974, County Down, Northern Ireland, UK) is a translator of Catullus, whom she admires for his clear diction, humour and flashes of unexpected hatred, all of which Flynn's poetry shares. But Flynn's themes are entirely different: motherhood, both from her own perspective as a single parent and that of her own mother; the strange fracturings of social media; elegy and death. Bernard O'Donoghue has described her as 'a good-humoured but devastating observer of the modern secular scene'.

Matthew Francis (b. 1956, Gosport, UK) started out as a writer of software manuals before turning to literature. It's difficult to imagine poems less like software manuals, delighting as they do in tall tales (as in 2008's *Mandeville*, a retelling of the unlikely journeys of the 14th-century adventurer), myth (as in his translation of the *Mabinogi*), and the shimmer and brilliance of the natural world (as in 2020's *Wing*, from which 'Ladybird Summer' is taken).

Isabel Galleymore (b. 1988, London, UK) was the first Poet in Residence at Tambopata Research Centre in the Amazon Rainforest. 'The opportunity to encounter different types of creature – spider monkeys, pink-toed tarantulas, caiman — was irresistible,' she writes; many of the poems in her debut collection, *Significant Other* (Carcanet, 2019), are the fruits of that opportunity. She is fascinated by the unusual in nature and by humanity's often difficult relationship with the natural world.

Alan Gillis (b. 1973, Belfast, Northern Ireland, UK) writes poems that are aware of the tension between the lyric and the mundane world. 'I do think that poets have to continually figure anew what to do with, say, the reality of class inequality, with contemporary banality, with the clichéd texture of our life – the way our wildest dreams now come optioned with brand names – within which we experience our real hurt and desire, fortitude and corruption.' He has explored this difficult terrain across five collections, most recently *The Readiness* (Picador Poetry, 2020).

Louise Glück (b. 1943, New York, USA), in her speech to the Swedish Academy, described the panic she felt when she was told that she'd won the Nobel Prize for Literature in October 2020: 'The light was too bright. The scale was too vast.' Instead, she envisages readers who come 'singly, one by one' and defends the privacy of the contact between writer and reader. Her poems make a space for that privacy; they are austere and expansive, returning to landscapes of meadowland, village and snowfall.

Rebecca Goss (b. 1974, Suffolk, UK) explores the female body with unflinching honesty, mediated through both trauma and celebration. The loss of her baby daughter is explored in her 2013 collection, *Her Birth*, and a long sequence responding to the work of artist Alison Watt is collected in *Girl* (Carcanet, 2019). Val McDermid has described Goss's poetry as 'precise and evocative, the images sharp as a photograph'.

Jorie Graham (b. 1950, New York, USA) was expelled from the Sorbonne for participating in the 1968 student protests. She has since published 16 collections of poems, most recently *Runaway* (Carcanet, 2020). Over the years, she has won the Pulitzer Prize, the Wallace Stevens Prize, the Nonino Prize and the 2012 Forward Prize for Best Collection. She teaches at Harvard. Her work is distinguished by characteristic long lines and jolts of syntax that illuminate the held objects suddenly and very brightly.

Lavinia Greenlaw (b. 1962, London, UK) was born into a family of scientists, and her poetry is remarkable for its clearness of perception and empirical eye. She's been Poet in Residence at the Science Museum and the Royal Society of Medicine, and she has also written novels, librettos and a 'sound work' for Manchester Piccadilly station (*Atlas Obscura*), which received the Ted Hughes Award for New Work in Poetry. Reviewing Greenlaw's most recent collection, *The Built Moment* (Faber & Faber, 2019), Sarah Crown praised 'a subtlety and an intellectual curiosity… that belies the wrench and rawness of the material'.

Jen Hadfield (b. 1978, Cheshire, UK) is fascinated by the strangeness of the natural world, in Shetland (where she lives) and further afield. As well as residences in the Shetland Library and at the Shetland Arts Trust, she has worked framing pictures and gutting fish. Her most recent collection is *The Stone Age* (Picador, 2021). 'It's to do with naming, though not in the sense of defining,' she writes about her own poetic process. 'And wanting to praise the land, and the fact that I am here and have gratitude for it.'

Nafeesa Hamid writes urgent, burning poems, tackling issues including mental health, domestic violence, gender, identity and culture. She's co-founder of the e-zine *Gully*, which works to platform the voices of South Asian writers and artists, and she runs a monthly spoken-word reading series in Derby, 'Twisted Tongues'. Her debut collection, *Besharam*, which translates as 'one who is shameless', bears witness to a traumatic abduction and assault; it was published by Verve Poetry Press in 2018.

Choman Hardi (b. 1974, Sulaymaniyah, Kurdistan, Iraq) came to the UK as a refugee in 1993. She initially wrote and published in Kurdish but turned to English for the detachment it allowed her when dealing with the difficult themes of her first collection, *Life For Us* (Bloodaxe Books, 2004): the Anfal genocide, statelessness and oppression. Hardi's poetry takes in atrocity but also celebrates resilience and community. In 2014, Hardi returned to her hometown of Sulaymaniyah to teach at the American University of Iraq.

Claire Harman (b. 1957, Guildford, UK) began her career in publishing at Carcanet Press and the poetry magazine *PN Review*, where she was co-ordinating editor in the 1980s. Her first book, a biography of the writer Sylvia Townsend Warner, was published in 1989. Four more literary biographies were followed by *Murder by the Book*, an account of a Victorian murder case, possibly provoked by an 1839 sensation novel. Her poem 'The Mighty Hudson' won the Forward Prize for Best Single Poem in 2015.

Will Harris (b. 1989, London, UK) writes, in the long essay *Mixed-Race Superman*, that 'the mixed-race person grows up to see the self as something strange and shifting'. Strange and shifting selves are at the heart of his first collection, *RENDANG* (Granta, 2020), which won the Forward Prize for Best First Collection. Reviewing it in the *Guardian*, Joanna Lee described how it 'leans into a vocabulary all of its own, and announces itself as an artefact that will not be dislodged' – a good metaphor for the way Harris's poems frequently build themselves around some lodged irritation, like the grain of sand which produces a pearl.

Seán Hewitt (b. 1990, Warrington, UK) took a university course on Old Irish poetry, which led him to the long poem *Buile Suibhne*; his translation of this poem into a series of 'lyric fragments' forms the heart of his debut collection, *Tongues of Fire* (Cape, 2020). Hewitt is a close observer of nature in its transience; his natural mode is the elegiac. In an interview with Jack Solloway, he says, 'I wanted *Tongues of Fire* to be ecological in the sense that everything is knitted into each poem, so that each poem would give you another glimpse at looking at grief or sex or whatever it was – and that those things are not separable.'

Selima Hill (b. 1945, London, UK) writes characteristic sequences of short, disturbing lyrics: each a brief glance, then a turning away, from a central subject, intimacy, violence or failed relationship. The poems are redeemed from bleakness by their surreal swerves from image to image, and by Hill's sense of humour, which is unlike anything else in contemporary poetry. She has published 20 collections since 1989, mostly with Bloodaxe Books. Fiona Sampson has described Hill's work as, 'of central importance in British poetry – not only for the courage of its subject matter but also for the lucid compression of its poetics'.

Ellen Hinsey (b. 1960, Boston, USA) is an independent researcher working at the crossroads of history, literature and politics. Her particular field of interest is totalitarianism and dissidence in Eastern Europe. This research feeds visibly into her poetry, especially her most recent collection, *The Illegal Age* (Arc Publications, 2018), a book-length sequence exploring 20th-century illiberalism which Marilyn Hacker has called 'a daring text – for its political acuity, and for its demonstration of the power in poetry to recount, remember, move the heart while opening the mind'.

Jane Hirshfield (b. 1953, New York, UK) is minimalist without being sparse: the short poems across her 12 collections are carefully attuned to the fullness and presence of what they describe, elements brought out by her Zen Buddhist training and ordination. 'I am interested in poems that find a clarity without simplicity,' Hirshfield has written; this interest has seen ecopoetic and scientific themes become more central to her work, and she has been Poet in Residence at a university neuroscience department and an experimental forest.

Sarah Howe (b. 1983, Hong Kong) came as a child to England, her father's country, but grew increasingly interested in the history of her mother, who was a refugee from Mao's China in 1949. She says that, for a long time, poetry was something she did 'under the radar of my official life as a university teacher and literary critic'. The poems in *Loop of Jade* (Chatto & Windus, 2014), the first debut collection to win the TS Eliot Prize, span a decade; the earliest are inspired by two journeys: her mother's journey as a baby and her own first trip to the Chinese mainland in 2004.

Clive James (b. 1939, Sydney, Australia) first came to popular attention as the television critic for the *Observer* in 1972; books of literary criticism, memoir and poetry followed, and he became a much-loved fixture on various ITV and BBC panel shows. Later in life, he turned his focus more centrally to poetry, translating Dante and writing several formally adept, elegiac collections. He died in November 2019.

Sarah James (b. 1975, Winchester, UK) plays with the possibilities of forms and technologies in her work; her online poem >*Room* is an exploration of a childhood diabetes diagnosis through words, images and hyperlinks. Likewise, many of the poems in *The Magnetic Diaries* (Knives Forks and Spoons, 2016) feature QR codes which allow readers to access multimedia elements in a 21st-century poetic reworking of *Madame Bovary*. The text was also turned into a one-act play for Hereford's Write On Festival.

Kathleen Jamie (b. 1962, Renfrewshire, Scotland, UK) wrote a poem to mark the 700th anniversary of the Battle of Bannockburn which is inscribed on a monument at the battle site. Questions of Scottish nationhood strongly inform her 10th collection, *The Bonniest Companie* (Picador Poetry, 2015), from which 'Blossom' is taken; Jamie wrote one poem a week in 2014, the year of the Scottish independence referendum, and the result is by turns tender, spontaneous and enraged. Jamie's earlier book, *The Tree House*, won the Forward Prize for Best Collection in 2004.

Jackie Kay (b. 1961, Edinburgh, Scotland, UK) was born to a Scottish mother and a Nigerian father, and was adopted as a baby by a white couple. Questions of identity and belonging animated her first collection, *The Adoption Papers* (Bloodaxe Books, 1991), which won the Scottish Arts Council Book of the Year. Kay is a novelist, playwright and children's author as well as a poet. In 2016, she was appointed Makar, the national poet for Scotland. Reviewing her most recent collection, *Bantam* (Picador Poetry, 2019), Kate Kellaway praised her poetry as 'loving, non-reverential and interested in the human predicament – in being quick not dead'.

Luke Kennard (b. 1981, Kingston-upon-Thames, UK) writes poems which are by turns tender and hilarious, playing with voice and tone. He can be disarmingly self-deprecating, but, as Caroline Bird writes, he 'has the uncanny genius of being able to stick a knife in your heart with such originality and verve that you start thinking "aren't knives fascinating… and hearts, my god!" whilst everything slowly goes black.' *Notes from the Sonnets* (Penned in the Margins, 2021) is his fifth collection.

Mimi Khalvati (b. 1944, Tehran, Iran) is the founder of the Poetry School, where she still teaches. After studying at Drama Centre London, she worked as an actor in the UK and a director in Tehran, before becoming a full-time freelance writer. She is a wide-ranging poet, hard to pin down to specific subjects (though images of her childhood at a boarding school on the Isle of Wight recur throughout her collections) or formal practices; she is as comfortable in free verse as she is in the measured stanzas of 'The Swarm', or in the sonnet sequence of her most recent collection, *Afterwardness* (Carcanet, 2019).

August Kleinzahler (b. 1949, Jersey City, USA) dropped out of university and hitchhiked from Wisconsin to Canada to study under Basil Bunting. His poems are choppy, fight-picking, alert to the rhythms of spoken language and with an unmistakable sense of place: especially the New Jersey shore, where he grew up, and San Francisco, where he now lives. In an interview, Kleinzahler describes how his poems set out deliberately to confuse 'readers who are more comfortable deciding at the top if this is a nice poem, or a pretty poem, or a sad poem, or an angry poem, whatever, and don't like the tablecloth to be pulled out from under them just as they're halfway through their Stroganoff'.

Neetha Kunaratnam (b. London, UK) interrogates the structures in society which justify war and inhumanity. His poetry casts an unflinching eye over narratives of masculinity, with a knack for quick, ironic character-drawing, whether of arms dealers, paintballing teenagers or suicide bombers. His debut collection, *Just Because*, was published by Smokestack Books in 2018; it contains 'The Afterlife', which won the Geoffrey Dearmer Prize in 2007.

James Lasdun (b. 1958, London, UK) has written in every imaginable genre: novels, short stories, scripts (including *Signs and Wonders*, starring Charlotte Rampling and Stellan Skarsgård), guidebooks and memoir. But his first successes were in poetry, to which he has always returned, most recently in *Water Sessions* (Cape Poetry, 2012). Lasdun is a master of the taut, hedged narrative, and James Wood has described him as 'one of the secret gardens of English literature'.

Hannah Lowe (b. 1976, Ilford, UK) is much haunted by genealogy and family history; she has pursued the mercurial figure of her father, a Chinese-black Jamaican migrant who made his living as a gambler, across two collections of poetry (taking their titles from her father's nicknames, *Chick* and *Chan*), and a memoir, *Long Time No See*. She's a poet of compassion and humour, evoking through sharp detail and cinematic technique a completely believable picture of mid-20th century London and Essex.

Lorraine Mariner (b. 1974, Upminster, UK) works as Assistant Librarian at the Poetry Library in the Southbank Centre. Above her desk is a quotation from the poet and conceptual artist George Brecht: 'There is so little to do and so much time to do it in.' It is a fitting motto for Mariner's work, which often takes its initial bearings from small familiarities –

assembling IKEA furniture, a child forgetting how to swim, a meal on the patio at dusk – before opening out into wider, stranger perspectives.

Glyn Maxwell (b. 1962, Welwyn Garden City, UK) is one of the few contemporary poets writing verse drama, a form whose requirements have fed back into his own work for the page: 'it's extremely helpful for the poet to hear how their lines sound through an actor's actual lungs. You can't get away with inauthenticity, you can't get away with stuff that tends to be cerebral, or too removed from reality,' he writes. Maxwell's long poem *Time's Fool* (Picador Poetry, 2000) is currently being adapted into a feature-length film.

Kei Miller (b. 1978, Kingston, Jamaica) enrolled in Creative Writing Poetry at the University of the West Indies because the Fiction course he wanted to take was full. 'I thought of poetry as just an exercise that would make me write better fiction, but it took over,' he says. *The Cartographer Tries to Map a Way to Zion*, his fourth poetry collection and the winner of the 2014 Forward Prize for Best Collection, was prompted by his realisation that 'maps pretend to be innocent but aren't'.

JO Morgan (b. 1978, Edinburgh, Scotland, UK) lives on a farm in the Scottish Borders and is the author of seven collections, each a single book-length poem or sequence. He is the son of a former RAF officer, who was involved in maintaining Britain's Airborne Nuclear Deterrent. *Assurances* (Cape Poetry, 2018), from which 'When he wakes…' is taken, is Morgan's response to his father's position: it eavesdrops on the thoughts of those trying to understand and justify their role in keeping peace by threatening war.

David Morley (b. 1964, Blackpool, UK) writes to give a voice to the voiceless or spoken-over. Many poems feature words of Angloromani, the mixed language spoken by British Romani; their anger is tempered by a sense of joy in the vast potentialities of speech and oral tradition. Morley grew up with a stammer, which he has described as a 'merciless muse': 'My teenage mind developed into a thesaurus of tensioned, alert possibility: hundreds of synonyms and antonyms allowed me to find the path of least resistance through sentences.'

Sinéad Morrissey (b. 1972, Portadown, Northern Ireland, UK) was Belfast's inaugural Poet Laureate. 'I knew I wanted to write poetry seriously, all my life, from the age of ten onwards,' she says; her poems are animated by a love of paradox and an eye for close, luminous detail. She has published six collections with Carcanet, including the 2013 TS Eliot Prize-winning collection *Parallax*, from which 'The Coal Jetty' is taken, and *On Balance*, which won the 2017 Forward Prize for Best Collection.

Paul Muldoon (b. 1951, Portadown, Northern Ireland, UK) was still a student when his first poetry collection, *New Weather*, was published by Faber & Faber. Later accolades would include the Pulitzer Prize and the role of Oxford Professor of Poetry, but perhaps the most memorable came in those early days from Seamus Heaney, to whom the young Muldoon showed a batch of poems with the question: what could be done to improve them? 'Nothing,' Heaney replied.

Les Murray (b. 1938, Nabiac, Australia) grew up in rural poverty on his grandparents' farm in Bunyah, which he would buy and return to in 1985. His poems take in an astonishing range of form and subject matter, a broadness of approach he celebrated in his great manifesto poem 'The Quality of Sprawl': 'Sprawl leans on things. It is loose-limbed in its mind. / Reprimanded and dismissed / it listens with a grin and one boot up on the rail / of possibility.' Murray was awarded the Queen's Gold Medal for Poetry in 1998; he died in April 2019.

Daljit Nagra (b. 1966, West Drayton, Hillingdon, UK) won the Forward Prize for Best First Collection, for *Look We Have Coming to Dover!* (Faber & Faber, 2007), three years after its title poem had won the Forward Prize for Best Single Poem. Nagra's central theme is British and Asian-British identity, in all its contradictions and complexities, whether explored via the rowdy, freewheeling monologues of his debut or the more sombre meditations of his latest collection, *British Museum* (Faber & Faber, 2017).

Sharon Olds (b. 1942, San Francisco, USA) was brought up in an abusive, Calvinistic household: her rejection of that upbringing informed the poems of her debut collection, 1980's *Satan Says*. She is drawn to taboo subjects and material from which other writers might flinch, and, besides her characteristic over-running lines, she rejects rhetorical or formal patterning. In an interview with Kaveh Akbar, Olds ties her writing back to the compulsion to tell human stories: 'not that we're trying to be moralists, because then we won't write well, but it has something to do with why our species isn't dead yet. We've had art to scare ourselves with.'

Alice Oswald (b. 1966, Reading, UK) recalls that she began writing poetry at age eight when, after a sleepless night, she found herself 'astonished by the clouds at dawn and realised they required a different kind of language.' This search for a different kind of language runs through her career; her subjects – whether water, flowers, insects or Agamemnon – never settle down and are never simply their present selves. Her second collection with Faber & Faber, *Dart*, which follows the River Dart from source to estuary, won the 2002 TS Eliot Prize.

Abigail Parry (b. 1983, UK) worked as a toymaker for seven years, and the poems in her debut collection, *Jinx* (Bloodaxe Books, 2018), bear a resemblance to dangerous toys or games: patterned surfaces, concealments, trick doors, sliding panels abound. She began thinking seriously about how poems worked when she read Maura Dooley's 'History' for the first time: 'It fascinated me: you could take it apart, like an engine, and examine every part to see what it was doing; at the same time, it worked a spell, and you can't see the joins in a spell.'

Don Paterson (b. 1963, Dundee, Scotland, UK) writes poems which are formally adept and emotionally devastating, while at the same time keeping one eye on their own workings; an ending which undercuts what has come before is a signature motif. His poems 'shine a light into crevices of feeling which amaze the poet as much as they move the reader,' wrote Helen Dunmore in the *Sunday Times*, reviewing *Landing Light* (Faber & Faber, 2003), which won both the Whitbread Prize for Poetry and the TS Eliot Prize.

Pascale Petit (b. 1963, Paris, France) was converted to poetry aged 16, when her teacher recited Keats' 'Ode to a Nightingale'. Her subsequent years as a sculptor and artist allowed her to develop connections between poetry and the visual and tactile arts, but her aim remained the same: like Keats, 'to create a forest the reader could walk into and see and hear even in the dark'. These imaginative landscapes range from the Amazonian rainforests of her early collections to the forests of Ranthambhore in Rajasthan, near her grandmother's birthplace, described in *Tiger Girl* (Bloodaxe Books, 2020).

Phoebe Power (b. 1993, Newcastle upon Tyne, UK) writes with close attention to place; her most recent publication is *Sea Change* (Guillemot, 2021), co-authored with Katherine Porteous in response to a residency on County Durham's 'radical coast'. The poems in *Shrines of Upper Austria* (Carcanet, 2018), from which 'notes on climate change' is taken and which won the Forward Prize for Best First Collection, take their bearings from the landscapes and local details of her grandmother's country, Austria, sometimes incorporating and assimilating entire lines of German among the English.

Shivanee Ramlochan (b. 1986, St. Joseph, Trinidad and Tobago) works as an arts journalist and blogger in Trinidad. Poetry for Ramlochan is a work of witness: the central sequence of her debut collection, *Everyone Knows I Am a Haunting* (Peepal Tree, 2018), 'The Red Thread Cycle', addresses and gives voice to survivors of sexual assault. The idea of a poem which says what it must, which speaks with its own unmistakable interior voice and leaves the poet 'awestruck and bewildered', is central to Ramlochan's practice as a writer.

Claudia Rankine (b. 1963, Kingston, Jamaica) decided against law school to pursue creative writing: 'Being a poet seemed like a risky career choice, but it felt like a calling – I didn't argue.' *Citizen* (Penguin Books, 2015), her fifth book, won the Forward Prize for Best Collection. The collage form of the collection is 'both archival and curatorial,' she says. It came about 'by asking friends to share their stories regarding interactions with either friends or colleagues'. Adam Fitzgerald describes her achievement in a *Guardian* review: 'To be able to plumb such innocent, overused words and make her readers find, inside their gaps and crevices, a whole world of familiar yet traumatic meanings.'

Vidyan Ravinthiran (b. 1984, Leeds, UK) was encouraged by his Sri Lankan parents to consider literature 'a wonderful thing'. He began writing poetry by creating versions of Keats' odes. This changed when he was given the 2002 Forward Book of Poetry by a friend of his mother. 'I had these old-fashioned ideas about what a poem should be,' Ravinthiran explains, 'and I couldn't square them with the excitements of free verse.' Ravinthiran has published two collections with Bloodaxe, *Grun-tu-Molani* (2014) and *The Million-Petalled Flower of Being Here* (2019).

Denise Riley (b. 1948, Carlisle, UK) is a philosopher and feminist theorist as well as an admired poet. She has written eight works of non-fiction, including the influential *'Am I That Name?': Feminism and the Category of "Women" in History*. From her first book, *Marxism for Infants*, through her astonishingly varied and ambitious *Mop Mop Georgette*, to the lyrical and elegiac *Say Something Back*, she has successfully sought to make abstract, intellectual questions vivid, pressing and personal.

Michael Symmons Roberts (b. 1963, Preston, UK) worked at the BBC as Executive Producer and Head of Development for BBC Religion & Ethics, before leaving to become a full-time writer. The sense of the spiritual in his writing manages to avoid getting bogged down in abstraction. Always his focus is on what is tangible; writing in the *Guardian*, Adam Newey praised his 'urge to find the immanent in the ordinary material world'. His long sonnet sequence *Drysalter* (Cape Poetry, 2013) won both the Forward Prize for Best Collection and the Costa Book Award for Poetry.

Roger Robinson (b. 1967, London, UK) is the lead vocalist for the band King Midas Sound. His fourth collection, *A Portable Paradise* (Peepal Tree, 2019), won the TS Eliot Prize. Robinson is a co-founder of the writing collective Malika's Poetry Kitchen, and of the workshop Spoke Lab, both of which work to create space in British culture for writers of colour. For Robinson, poets 'can translate trauma into something people can face. Sometimes there's a cost for the poet to do that as it takes looking at the trauma right in the face and then allowing others to bear the idea of trauma safely.' He has described his own poems, memorably, as 'empathy machines'.

Stephen Santus (b. 1948, Wigan, UK) has been writing poetry since 1965. His interest was sparked by his older brother who loved to read poetry and Shakespeare aloud. Santus appreciates classical Chinese poets and the Japanese haiku and tanka writers for their delicacy and emotional accessibility. He teaches English in a language school in Oxford, having previously taught in France and Austria. 'In a Restaurant', entered by a mystery admirer, won the Forward Prize for Best Single Poem in 2014.

Stephen Sexton (b. 1988, Belfast, Northern Ireland, UK) spent a lot of time when he was nine years old playing Super Mario World. His debut collection *If All the World and Love Were Young* (Penguin Books), which won the 2019 Forward Prize for Best First Collection, remaps the pastoral tradition onto familiar Nintendo landscapes; like Milton's 'Lycidas', it is a pastoral elegy, in this case for the poet's mother. Starting to write, he 'soon realised that this particular game was so much a part of my childhood that I couldn't write about it without thinking of my childhood, and I couldn't write about my childhood without thinking of grief'.

Jo Shapcott (b. 1953, London, UK) writes about change and transformation; the titles of both her fifth collection, *Of Mutability* (Faber & Faber, 2010), and her collection of lectures on poetry, *The Transformers* (Bloodaxe Books, 2018), are characteristic. Equally distinctive is her engagement with the scientific: 'Any distinctive language interests me, whether it's that of football or knitting, but scientific language is very beautiful. Each word opens a world,' she writes.

Danez Smith (b. 1989, St Paul, Minnesota, USA) is African-American, queer, gender-neutral and HIV positive. They first became aware of the possibilities of contemporary poetry through HBO's 'Def Poetry' and honed their performance skills with theatre training and slams. (Smith is the reigning Rustbelt Individual Champion.) The poems which excite them most, they say, are those which 'through language, better equip me to re-enter the world and proceed vigorously'. Their second collection, *Don't Call Us Dead* (Chatto & Windus), won the Forward Prize for Best Collection in 2018.

Tracy K Smith (b. 1972, Falmouth, Massachusetts, USA) was the Poet Laureate of the United States from 2017 to 2019. She began writing poems aged 10, but it was not until she lost her mother to cancer at 22 that poetry became, in her words, 'a tool for living'. In 2012 she won the Pulitzer Prize for *Life on Mars* – a collection she has described as 'looking out to the universe and forward to an imagined future'; *Wade in the Water*, by contrast, looks 'earthward and backward', confronting unflinchingly the moral crises of race and history in America.

Jean Sprackland (b. 1962, Burton-on-Trent, UK) pays attention to the histories concealed in objects; in her fourth collection, *Sleeping Keys* (Cape Poetry, 2013), the collapse of a marriage is narrated through the close survey of a house. Her non-fiction, too, explores what's often overlooked; one collection of essays meditates on beach detritus, another on untidy graveyards. Sprackland won the Costa Book Award for Poetry for *Tilt* (Cape Poetry) in 2007.

Martha Sprackland (b. 1988, Barnstaple, UK) was six when she met her future publisher, Deryn Rees-Jones, at a poetry workshop for children in Sefton Park. (She wrote a poem about a mouse, on purple sugar-paper, with a felt-tip pen.) She worked as poetry editor at *Poetry London*, and in 2017 she co-founded her own small press, Offord Road Books. The poems in *Citadel* (Pavilion Poetry, 2020), from which 'Pimientos de Padrón' is taken, enter into an eerie, intimate dialogue with the 16th-century Queen of Spain, Juana de Castilla.

Julian Stannard (b. 1962, Kent, UK) has a genius for titles: recent publications include *What Were You Thinking?* (CB Editions, 2016) and *Average is the New Fantastico* (Green Bottle, 2019). His poems are witty and urbane, occasionally displaying, as in 'Trolley Man', flashes of gleeful menace. He is a Reader in English and Creative Writing at the University of Winchester, and is currently working on a history of transatlantic poetry between 1945 and 2015.

Arundhathi Subramaniam (b. 1973, Mumbai, India) is a writer on spirituality and culture as well as being a poet, with a background in dance. 'I am fascinated by the way in which a Bharata Natyam dancer invokes the sacred without sacrificing groundedness – the way she reaches for the sublime without ever losing a sensuous connection with the earth,' she writes. 'That's the way I see the lyric poem – as a kind of verbal connection between earth and sky.' Her 2015 collection, *When God is a Traveller*, won the first Khushwant Singh Memorial Prize for Poetry.

George Szirtes (b. 1948, Budapest, Hungary) came to England as a refugee after the 1956 Hungarian uprising. He originally trained as a painter, but while studying at the Leeds College of Art and Design, he was simultaneously perfecting his verse technique. For Szirtes, 'Rhyme… helps us stick the world together while all the time drawing attention to its own fabricated nature.' He is deftly formal but never at the expense of warmth and connection. Bloodaxe Books brought together his first dozen collections in 2008's *New and Collected Poems*: four new volumes have followed since then, most recently *Fresh out of the Sky*, in 2021.

Maria Taylor (b. 1978, Worksop, UK) finds her subject matter in unexpected places and scenarios: Daniel Craig appears in a married woman's bed; a matador reminisces about Hemingway; the ghost of a murdered actor roams Covent Garden. *Dressing for the Afterlife* (Nine Arches Press, 2020) is her second collection. Kathy Pimlott has praised 'her extravagantly vagrant thought paths', which lure the reader on 'to follow fancy into unsettling and exhilarating territory'.

Kae Tempest (b. 1985, London, UK) started performing at open mic nights when they were 16; before releasing a debut collection, they had toured with John Cooper Clarke, Billy Bragg and Benjamin Zephaniah. Fusing elements from spoken word and hip-hop traditions, Tempest is an electrifying live performer. Their poems and plays often subvert or update Ancient Greek mythology; in Tempest's words, the myths 'remind us that every person, every passer-by on the street, has an "epic narrative" within'.

Lucy Anne Watt (b. 1951, Hampshire, UK) is a novelist as well as a poet; *Micawber's Ailment* was published in 1992 by the Women's Press. Her poetry benefits from a novelist's eye for character, as in the grieving mother of 'The Tree Position', her son killed in the Middle East. The critic Wolfgang Görtschacher praised the poem in his *Companion to Contemporary British and Irish Poetry* as demonstrating the strength of poetry written out of 'the solidarity of mothers'.

Hugo Williams (b. 1942, Windsor, UK) first wrote poetry aged 13, copying Laurie Lee and the Movement poets. 'I liked writing,' he says, 'because I could do it and it cheered me up.' Poetry, for Williams, is an opportunity to say the unsayable, 'a search for meaning rather than an extension of existing thoughts'. An extended dialysis treatment and a brush with mortality formed the subject matter for some of the poems in Williams' 11th collection, *I Knew the Bride* (Faber & Faber, 2014).

Luke Wright (b. 1982, London, UK) is a founder member of the poetry collective Aisle16. He has created nine solo shows for his own extended poems, most recently a sequence of rewritten Georgian street ballads. Since 2006, Wright has curated the Latitude Festival's Poetry Arena. George Szirtes has described his work as 'not only verbally substantial, skillful and very funny, but also complex in its feeling.'

Publisher acknowledgements

The poems in this anthology are reprinted from the following books. Every effort has been made to trace the copyright holders of the poems published in this anthology. The publisher apologises if any material has been included without permission, or without the appropriate acknowledgement, and would be glad to be told of anyone who has not been consulted.

Thanks are due to all the copyright holders for their kind permission:

Patience Agbabi · The Doll's House · *The Poetry Review*
Mir Mahfuz Ali · Hurricane · *Midnight, Dhaka* · Seren
Raymond Antrobus · The Perseverance · *The Perseverance* · Penned in the Margins
Simon Armitage · Poundland · *Paper Aeroplane: Selected Poems 1989–2014* · Faber & Faber
Mona Arshi · What Every Girl Should Know Before Marriage · *Small Hands* · Pavilion Poetry
Fatimah Asghar · Partition · *If They Come for Us* · Corsair, Little, Brown Book Group
Fiona Benson · Eurofighter Typhoon · *Vertigo & Ghost* · Cape Poetry
Tara Bergin · Stag-Boy · *This is Yarrow* · Carcanet
Emily Berry · Aura · *Stranger, Baby* · Faber & Faber
Liz Berry · The Republic of Motherhood · *Granta*
Sujata Bhatt · Poppies in Translation · *Poppies in Translation* · Carcanet
Caroline Bird · Rookie · *The Air Year* · Carcanet
Malika Booker · The Little Miracles · *Magma Poetry*
Sean Borodale · 10th February: Queen · *Bee Journal* · Cape Poetry
Colette Bryce · Derry · *The Whole & Rain-domed Universe* · Picador Poetry
John Burnside · On the Vanishing of My Sister, Aged 3, 1965 · *All One Breath* · Cape Poetry
Niall Campbell · The Night Watch · *Noctuary* · Bloodaxe Books
Vahni Capildeo · Investigation of Past Shoes · *Measures of Expatriation* · Carcanet

Mary Jean Chan · The Window · *Flèche* · Faber & Faber

Brendan Cleary · It's Our Dance · *Face* · Pighog

Loretta Collins Klobah · Peckham, London, Cold Water Flat · *The Twelve-Foot Neon Woman* · Peepal Tree

David Constantine · The Rec · *Elder* · Bloodaxe Books

Robert Crawford · Herakleitos · *Testament* · Cape Poetry

Emily Critchley · Something wonderful has happened it is called you · *Ten Thousand Things* · Boiler House Press

Nichola Deane · Yesterday's Child · *Trieste* · Smith I Doorstop

Tishani Doshi · Girls Are Coming Out of the Woods · *Girls Are Coming Out of the Woods* · Bloodaxe Books

Sarah Doyle · The woman who married an alchemist · *The Fenland Reed*

Nick Drake · Through the Red Light · *Out of Range* · Bloodaxe Books

Carol Ann Duffy · Empty Nest · *Empty Nest* · Picador Poetry · Copyright © Carol Ann Duffy · Reproduced by permission of the author c/o Rogers, Coleridge & White Ltd

Ian Duhig · Bridled Vows · *The Blind Roadmaker* · Picador Poetry

Kate Edwards · Frequency Violet · *Ink Sweat & Tears*

Rhian Edwards · Skype · *Clueless Dogs* · Seren

Helen Farish · A Night in at Nohant · *Nocturnes at Nohant* · Bloodaxe Books

Paul Farley · The Power · *The Dark Film* · Picador Poetry

Parwana Fayyaz · Forty Names · *PN Review*

Vicki Feaver · The Larder · *I Want! I Want!* · Cape Poetry

Leontia Flynn · The Radio · *Poetry Ireland Review*

Matthew Francis · Ladybird Summer · *Wing* · Faber & Faber

Isabel Galleymore · The Starfish · *Significant Other* · Carcanet

Alan Gillis · Bulletin from The Daily Mail · *Scapegoat* · The Gallery Press

Louise Glück · An Adventure · *Faithful and Virtuous Night* · Carcanet

Rebecca Goss · Stretch Marks · *Her Birth* · Carcanet/Northern House

Jorie Graham · Tree · *London Review of Books*

Lavinia Greenlaw · The break · *The Built Moment* · Faber & Faber

Jen Hadfield · Definitions · *Byssus* · Picador Poetry

Nafeesa Hamid · Doctor's appointment · *Besharam* · Verve Poetry Press

Choman Hardi · Dispute Over a Mass Grave · *Considering the Women* · Bloodaxe Books

Claire Harman · The Mighty Hudson · *Times Literary Supplement*

Will Harris · SAY · *The Poetry Review*

Seán Hewitt · October · *Tongues of Fire* · Cape Poetry

Selima Hill · The Elephant is Much Too Big to Boogie · *People Who Like Meatballs* · Bloodaxe Books

Ellen Hinsey · Evidence THE LAWS · *The Illegal Age* · Arc Publications

Jane Hirshfield · The Supple Deer · *Come, Thief* · Bloodaxe Books

Sarah Howe · (c) Tame · *Loop of Jade* · Chatto & Windus

Clive James · Holding Court · *Times Literary Supplement*

Sarah James · Monday, 12th August: Secrets · *The Magnetic Diaries* · Knives Forks and Spoons

Kathleen Jamie · Blossom · *The Bonniest Companie* · Picador Poetry

Jackie Kay · Vault · *Bantam* · Picador Poetry

Luke Kennard · Crow Baby · *The Scores*

Mimi Khalvati · The Swarm · *The Poetry Review*

August Kleinzahler · Epistle xxxix · *The Hotel Oneira* · Faber & Faber

Neetha Kunaratnam · The Afterlife · *Just Because* · Smokestack Books

James Lasdun · Stones · *Water Sessions* · Cape Poetry

Hannah Lowe · Dance Class · *Chick* · Bloodaxe Books

Lorraine Mariner · Strangers · *There Will Be No More Nonsense* · Picador Poetry

Glyn Maxwell · The Byelaws · *One Thousand Nights & Counting: Selected Poems* · Picador Poetry

Kei Miller · Establishing the Metre · *The Cartographer Tries to Map a Way to Zion* · Carcanet

JO Morgan · When he wakes... · *Assurances* · Cape Poetry

David Morley · FURY · *FURY* · Carcanet

Sinéad Morrissey · The Coal Jetty · *Parallax* · Carcanet

Paul Muldoon · Pelt · *One Thousand Things Worth Knowing* · Faber & Faber

Les Murray · High-speed Bird · *Taller When Prone* · Carcanet

Daljit Nagra · A Black History of the English-Speaking Peoples · *Tippoo Sultan's Incredible White-Man-Eating Tiger Toy-Machine!!!* · Faber & Faber

Sharon Olds · Departure Gate Aria · *Arias* · Cape Poetry

Alice Oswald · Slowed-Down Blackbird · *Falling Awake* · Cape Poetry

Abigail Parry · The Quilt · *Jinx* · Bloodaxe Books

Don Paterson · Mercies · *40 Sonnets* · Faber & Faber

Pascale Petit · Green Bee-eater · *Tiger Girl* · Bloodaxe Books

Phoebe Power · notes on climate change · *Shrines of Upper Austria* ·
Carcanet

Shivanee Ramlochan · On the Third Anniversary of the Rape · *Everyone
Knows I Am a Haunting* · Peepal Tree

Claudia Rankine · The New Therapist Specializes... · *Citizen: An
American Lyric* · Penguin Books

Vidyan Ravinthiran · A Chair Addresses Jackie Chan · *Grun-tu-molani* ·
Bloodaxe Books

Denise Riley · After La Rochefoucauld · Eggbox/UEA Poetry Series

Michael Symmons Roberts · Footfall · *Drysalter* · Cape Poetry

Roger Robinson · Trinidad Gothic · *The Butterfly Hotel* · Peepal Tree

Stephen Santus · In a Restaurant · Bridport Prize

Stephen Sexton · Front Door · *If All the World and Love Were Young* ·
Penguin Books

Jo Shapcott · Bees · *The Poetry Review*

Danez Smith · dinosaurs in the hood · *Don't Call Us Dead* ·
Chatto & Windus

Tracy K Smith · Annunciation · *Wade in the Water* · Penguin Books

Jean Sprackland · Shepherdess and Swain · *The North Magazine*

Martha Sprackland · Pimientos de Padrón · *Citadel* · Pavilion Poetry

Julian Stannard · Trolley Man · *Heat Wave* · Salt Publishing

Arundhathi Subramaniam · My Friends · *When God is a Traveller* ·
Bloodaxe Books

George Szirtes · Actually, Yes · *Bad Machine* · Bloodaxe Books

Maria Taylor · Loop · *Dressing for the Afterlife* · Nine Arches Press

Kae Tempest · Thirteen · *Hold Your Own* · Picador Poetry

Lucy Anne Watt · The Tree Position · Torbay Open Poetry Competition

Hugo Williams · From the Dialysis Ward · *Collected Poems* ·
Faber & Faber

Luke Wright · To London... · *What I Learned from Johnny Bevan* ·
Penned in the Margins

Winners of the Forward Prizes 2011–2020

Best Collection

2020 · Caroline Bird · *The Air Year* · Carcanet
2019 · Fiona Benson · *Vertigo & Ghost* · Cape Poetry
2018 · Danez Smith · *Don't Call Us Dead* · Chatto & Windus
2017 · Sinéad Morrissey · *On Balance* · Carcanet
2016 · Vahni Capildeo · *Measures of Expatriation* · Carcanet
2015 · Claudia Rankine · *Citizen: An American Lyric* · Penguin Books
2014 · Kei Miller · *The Cartographer Tries to Map a Way to Zion* · Carcanet
2013 · Michael Symmons Roberts · *Drysalter* · Cape Poetry
2012 · Jorie Graham · *PLACE* · Carcanet
2011 · John Burnside · *Black Cat Bone* · Cape Poetry

Best First Collection

2020 · Will Harris · *RENDANG* · Granta Poetry
2019 · Stephen Sexton · *If All the World and Love Were Young* · Penguin Books
2018 · Phoebe Power · *Shrines of Upper Austria* · Carcanet
2017 · Ocean Vuong · *Night Sky with Exit Wounds* · Cape Poetry
2016 · Tiphanie Yanique · *Wife* · Peepal Tree
2015 · Mona Arshi · *Small Hands* · Pavilion Poetry
2014 · Liz Berry · *Black Country* · Chatto & Windus
2013 · Emily Berry · *Dear Boy* · Faber & Faber
2012 · Sam Riviere · *81 Austerities* · Faber & Faber
2011 · Rachael Boast · *Sidereal* · Picador Poetry

Best Single Poem

2020 · Malika Booker · The Little Miracles · *Magma*
2019 · Parwana Fayyaz · Forty Names · *PN Review*
2018 · Liz Berry · The Republic of Motherhood · *Granta*
2017 · Ian Patterson · The Plenty of Nothing · *PN Review*
2016 · Sasha Dugdale · Joy · *PN Review*
2015 · Claire Harman · The Mighty Hudson · *Times Literary Supplement*
2014 · Stephen Santus · In a Restaurant · Bridport Prize
2013 · Nick MacKinnon · The Metric System · *The Warwick Review*
2012 · Denise Riley · A Part Song · *London Review of Books*
2011 · RF Langley · To a Nightingale · *London Review of Books*

Supporting Poetry with Forward

Proceeds from the sale of this book benefit the charity Forward
Arts Foundation. Forward believes everyone should have the
opportunity to develop creativity and agency by making, experiencing
and sharing poetry.

We aim to promote public knowledge, understanding and enjoyment
of poetry in the UK and Ireland. We are committed to widening
poetry's audience, honouring achievement and supporting talent.
Our programmes include National Poetry Day, the Forward Prizes
for Poetry and the Forward Book of Poetry, an annual anthology of
the year's best poems.

Our mission is:
- To celebrate excellence in poetry
- To increase poetry's audience
- To deepen appreciation of poetry's role

To find out more about our work and for further reading about the
Forward Prizes' alumni, visit our website forwardartsfoundation.org and
follow us on Facebook or Twitter @ForwardPrizes.